When Katrina Stood Down
We Came Running,
But Rita Tripped Us

When Katrina Stood Down
We Came Running,
But Rita Tripped Us

Shandra Love

E-BookTime, LLC
Montgomery, Alabama

When Katrina Stood Down We Came Running,
But Rita Tripped Us

Library of Congress Control Number: 2006928249

ISBN: 978-1-59824-268-3

First Edition
Published May 2006
E-BookTime, LLC
6598 Pumpkin Road
Montgomery, AL 36108
www.e-booktime.com

Acknowledgments

I'd like to thank the noted survivors of Hurricanes Katrina and Rita, for allowing me to put a name, a face and emotions to the devastation that was caused by both.

Never in my wildest dream would I believe that I would be compelled to go behind the scenes to witness the misery, anguish and despair that got them in a choke hold and held them hostage.

Even farther from my thoughts was the possibility that I would soon be seeking shelter from a storm.

Bridget and Keith C., Kiwana B., Jerry, Mya, Lena, Marvin, Melvin, Brittney, Ron, Celestine, Ella, Terrance, Rose, Nancy, Mary Jones and son Karl (double evacuees) Jose' Castro, Theresa W. (double evacuee), Isaiah and Deborah Johnson, Harriett Butler, Donald - my off the chain "foot massager," Sybil and husband from Port Arthur.

I'm grateful that you have shared and have allowed me to share your stories with those who care to know them. God speed in your new beginnings and for the opportunity to serve and get to know you.

Special 'shouts' to these fellow relief workers:

Bren, Nissie, Smokie, Tina, Blue, Jasmine, Trenika, Mary E., Cly, Thomasene, Kathy B., and the many others who were willing to do whatever needed to be done in order to bring much needed encouragement and support to our brothers and sisters who found themselves to be "strangers" in their own land.

Sincere thanks to E. Claudette Freeman and Bishop Victor T. Curry, who allowed me an on-air interview on radio station WMBM, in North Miami, Florida.

The response from your listeners was overwhelming. Their blessings from the heart allowed me to *extend help beyond the threshold of my immediate community.*

Numerous churches and individuals were able to reap the benefits of this kind deed. May God continue to keep you in His "Perfect Will."

I would also like to thank my own pastor, Superintendent Eddie Toppen, Jr., for saying, "Yes" to the numerous thoughts or ideas that I presented to him.

Outside of my biological father, no man has ever had a greater impact or presence in my life. May our "Heavenly Father" continue to keep you in the word and freely reeling in 'lost' souls.

In saving the best for last, I'd like to bestow the highest accolades possible on my beautiful (inside and out) mother J. R. P. a.k.a. "Minnie." You did all that you were supposed to do the rest is on me.

~ As usual, what you see is what you get. I won't be doing any extra. Try to enjoy it anyway. ~

To "Gloria," I did it anyway didn't I? Thank you!
~Smile~

Foreword

First and foremost, I'd like to give thanks to God, for all that He has done and all that He has allowed to come about, in spite of the devastating wrath of Hurricanes Katrina and Rita.

With Katrina hitting the areas of Louisiana, Mississippi and Alabama on August 29, 2005, and Rita hitting Texas, Louisiana and other coastal areas in the early morning hours of September 24, 2005, many lives were lost, many people were displaced and countless more were left at the mercy of 'strangers.'

The nation struggled to come to grips with one of the worst natural disasters to strike in an extremely long time and we weren't even remotely prepared. No one could anticipate the ramifications thereof. Not to mention that Rita caught us all sleeping. Dare we awake?

This book will not focus solely on the powers that be or how they managed to let these hurricanes "sneak in" and exact such a deadly revenge, nor whose fault it ultimately was that a good number perished after Katrina blew through these areas.

Instead, it will enlighten you to my experience as a Hurricane Relief Volunteer (who worked directly with evacuees) and their own stories.

This will be as it was told to me and as I witnessed it for myself. Their identities have been changed (with the exception of those who want it to be known who they are), but their stories are real.

I pray that it allows you to tap into their anguish, grief and sense of hopelessness as the blame game and sensationalism took center stage.

This experience has shaken me beyond belief and I know that as a result I'll never be the same.

Chapter One

"Girl, you know we have to get down there tomorrow and help those people from Louisiana." I awaited her response and hoped that it would be what I wanted to hear.

I didn't know a lot about getting to some of the more well known places in Houston, but come heck or high water, I was going to get to any or all of the facilities that were housing the Hurricane Katrina evacuees.

"Help who? You talking 'bout the ones from New Orleans?" Nissie is a mess. She has a way of turning the most crucial of events into a moment of gut busting laughter. When I composed myself I answered.

"Yeah girl. I've been keeping tabs on what Houston was going to be doing for them and the food bank needs volunteers to come in and sort, bag and deliver the groceries to the various locations that are assisting the evacuees." I said.

"What times are they wanting help? Where is the food bank anyway?" she inquired. I reached for my tablet and started in. "They'll be needing help from 8-12 and 1-5 tomorrow, from 1-5 on Saturday, and 8-12 and 1-5 on Monday, which will be Labor Day."

"Well, I'd much rather get it out of the way and do it from 8-12. Would that be cool for you too? It ain't too early, huh?" she asked.

"Naw, that's fine with me. Be sure to round up your crew. With all seventy-five of y'all, that time could be cut considerably." We laughed pretty hard on that because we knew I was telling the truth.

Nissie and Bren are sisters. They each have three children and a plethora of nieces, nephews, cousins, in-laws and people in between.

Whenever they put their minds to something, they come out in force. They tickle me, because they make a fuss here and there, but for the most part they'll back you one thousand percent whenever you ask their assistance with something.

"Girl, I'm at work and my break has just ended, let me get back with you when I get in later tonight. In the meantime start rounding up the posse so we can get in there and knock it on out. OK?"

She ended it with a quick utterance of, "Okie dokie," and we were off the phone. I jotted down another facility that needed volunteers and headed out the door.

I was at home responding to e-mail and making contact with organizations throughout the area, when she called.

The usual "Hey" greeted me. "Hey, what's up? Were you able to round up any of ya' people?" I asked. She cleared her throat and said, "Yeah, Bren and Smokie are going with us. So what will we have to do? Are there a lot of other people who'll be there, too?" she asked.

I tried to gather my thoughts without glancing over at my notes and said, "There will be other volunteers there and we will be grouping, sorting and delivering food items."

"Oh, but we won't actually be with or around any of the actual evacuees?" she sounded a tad bit disappointed.

"No, they aren't housing them. They're only handling the food that's being donated." I answered. "OK, well call me in the morning when you get up and start moving around." 'In the morning' rolled around a lot sooner than anticipated.

"Heyyy, You up yet?" I asked the first voice that answered the phone. "Yeah, you looking for Nissie? This is Blue."

I was so embarrassed. I didn't want to disturb anyone but her. "Awww girl, I'm sorry that I woke you up. I thought your crazy mother might be near the phone. Is she up?"

She laughed and said, "It's OK, hold on, let me get her. Niss-saaaay! It's Sister Shandra." After a few minutes she stumbled to the phone. I shook my head and laughed.

Knowing her, she had probably only gotten to bed about two hours prior to my calling.

I cut straight to the chase and asked, "Hey girl what's up? You ready to roll out?" She cleared her throat and said, "Yeah." I teased her for a minute because I didn't believe her and then said, "Cool. Who else is going to go with us?"

"Tina and Jasmine are going and should be over here by seven. You said they start at eight, right? Then Trenika, Smokie, and Bren are going, so there'll be seven of us in all."

"That'll work. Well, I'll be on my way over there in about fifteen minutes. Listen for me." We got off and I finished getting dressed and making sure I had covered all bases before leaving home.

Blue was the one to let me in. She was a little amazed that we early birds were up and about already. She had been washing and folding clothes. It was a good time for her to part with things that she could live without and she seemed to want to do it while the energy levels were high.

She knew someone who had taken in several evacuees and she wanted to be sure that they got a good amount of the clothing that they were getting rid of.

"Miss Shandra you act like you be up moving around like this all of the time. Do you?" she asked. I laughed and responded, "Now you know I'm an insomniac. Sleep is *not* my friend."

She shook her head and smacked her lips, "Girrrl, How do you do it? How can you function? When do you sleep?"

"Blue, to be honest, I'm on 'Automatic Pilot' most of the time. I sleep when it comes to me, if I'm at home. If I'm elsewhere, I have to fight it."

I sat down and started watching the news about Katrina. The gentleman who had his wife to lose his grip was being interviewed. They were doing an update showing that someone in Georgia had given him a home to live in.

It was already getting to me so I went into the kitchen to see what might be available for me to eat. I had been doing a lot of 'skip eating' and it was throwing me out of sync.

"Blue, you coulda had a turkey sammich in here for me. A slice of turkey bacon or sum'n would have been fine. What's up with that? How you gone have somebody over at 'cho house and not feed 'em?" I called to her from the kitchen.

She chuckled and said, "Sister Shandra, you know I don't cook." Nissie walked in and shared that she had some turkey ham in the refrigerator and was a little disappointed when we went through and found that it was gone.

I cracked a half dozen eggs and added shredded cheese, milk, and salt and pepper. I had it going real nice. Blue slid through and told me to make enough for her, Bren and Smokie, too.

Trenika asked that I make her one. We were quite outdone when Bren and Smokie came in finishing off their hot link sandwiches. I told them I wouldn't be cooking for them again anytime soon.

Tina and Jasmine rolled in a little after Bren and Smokie, but before we left I called the food bank to be sure that they still needed help. I was glad that I did.

The person answering the phone stated that there were so many there already, that they didn't need anyone else. She did offer up the Salvation Army and Second Baptist Church, since they were doing the required training for "Operation Compassion."

I got those numbers and called to see when and where we might be able to get in and start helping people today. Training would be taking place at Second Baptist Church at 9:00 a.m. and we had just enough time to make it, if we left right away.

We ran out into the cars and headed that way. Anyone completing the training would be working as Food Relief Workers at the George R. Brown Convention Center.

"Operation Compassion" would also be providing personal hygiene kits to evacuees. The two-hour training would prepare us for what was to be expected and what we would absolutely, positively have to do when serving food items to the evacuees. This is required training from the state and there was no cutting corners on it. If you didn't take the course, you couldn't serve food, plain and simple.

Upon arriving at the church, we were floored with seeing so many different people filing in, ready, willing and able to assist in this effort.

They were Black, White, Hispanic, Sri Lankan, Chinese, Japanese and many other ethnic groups that escape me.

They were young, middle aged, older. We seemed to all be stepping quickly and deliberately, knowing we had a purpose.

We filled out paper work and an information sheet that we could keep handy and refer back to. After it ended and we were made aware that we could check online for any assignments given us, we set out and wondered how we'd spend the rest of the day since we were in a mood to work.

I suggested that we ride over to the Astrodome area since we knew that many of them had been sleeping out over there and could possibly use our help.

"You wanna go down there just so you won't be able to get in, huh?" Bren asked. I laughed and said, "Naw girl, they're not all inside the arena. We can go down there and see if we can talk to some of them and see if there is anything that we can do for them." I said.

Nissie chimed in with, "Now if they're out and about like they say on the news, we'll be able to find out what they need right now and try to help them with that."

"Well, if we're going come on. It's sprinkling and I don't want to be getting wet while we decide." Smokie was the one who offered up this bit of advice.

She's a mover and shaker. She was ready at time, on time, be the time, all the time. She was not one to be sitting up and waiting on folk to make their minds up.

We loaded up and headed for the Astrodome. At first we weren't sure that we'd be able to see them, but as we got closer, there they were. Some were sitting under trees, others were standing in the parking lot and others were walking to and from, on a mission.

Some walked with their heads down, while others wanted, needed for everyone to see them, to remember their faces and plight.

The traffic congestion was unbearable. Flashing signs directed volunteers to other parking lots and made us aware that no donations were being accepted at the site.

The people who looked at us as we passed them seemed grateful for the sympathetic smiles and understanding waves of our hands.

My moment was broken when Bren asked, "Are y'all trying to go up in there? I don't feel like wrestling with anyone in a parking space or trying to get out."

We kind of looked around at one another and agreed that the heavy traffic and foot patrol of other volunteers was something we didn't want to deal with, if we just didn't have to.

"Why don't you just park in one of the parking lots of one of the stores and we can walk around here and do what we're going to do?" Nissie suggested.

"OK. Let me see where I can park. There's a Fiesta over there and a little strip center over here…" Nissie interrupted with, "Look, there's a Toys-R-Us down there. Let's go see what they have in there. Maybe we can find the babies some toys."

A big orange sign gave notice that a donation site had been moved and was now operating about a half block away at an old Garden Ridge Pottery store. From the looks of it, one of the fire departments was sponsoring this drive.

We went ahead into Toys-R-Us and started perusing the many things that they had available. Nissie was in heaven. This was her type of thing. She was pulling out all kinds of stuff and playing with it.

Smokie sighed and said, "Y'all knew better than to bring her in here." Tina, who had been rather quiet, showed her sign of agreement by easing in a little "Humph."

Trenika found a stuffed horse and was pretending to ride it when Jasmine came over and said, "Granny give me some money, those boys asked me for a dollar."

We all found ourselves looking in the direction that she was pointing and the two boys, who looked to be about eleven and nine, were walking down an aisle.

We were in our purses and pockets trying to find some odd pieces of change to give to them and after digging up a few dollars, Jasmine, Trenika and I would go looking for them.

When we caught up with them a man was talking to them. I didn't want to intrude or embarrass them, but I did want to be sure that he meant well.

Call it 'motherly instinct,' but I wasn't going to move outside of earshot until I was comfortable with what he was saying to them.

As it turns out, he was a generous young man who was getting them a toy. After he walked away I asked them, "Were y'all needing a couple of dollars to grab a bite to eat?"

They slyly looked over at one another. The older one replied, "Yes ma'am." I counted out the singles and divided them evenly between them.

"OK, be sure you get something that's going to fill you up and don't venture off from the center too far by yourselves, OK?" I cautioned.

At the same time they said, "We won't. Thank you." I wanted to know a little more and asked, "Who are you here with? Did all of you get here OK?"

Again it was the older one who would answer. "I'm with about eighteen of my cousins." I was glad to hear that, but when he added, "I don't know where my mother is though," it was all over for me.

I knew I couldn't react in front of him, but I could feel the tears coming. I hugged both of them and said, "You know it's going to be all right though, don't you?"

He smiled and said, "Yes ma'am." Before they walked away I asked if they were cousins, it would be the younger one who would speak. He halfway grinned and said, "We are *now*."

Their stale little bodies tickled my nose, but it was by no means important to me, only that they seemed oblivious to the trauma that seemed to be plaguing the older evacuees.

Jasmine and Trenika had already started a slow walk back to where the rest of them were. They were fully involved and crying.

I hadn't done any better. Knowing that this baby was in another city, with his mother's whereabouts being unknown to him caused me a high level of distress.

One of the workers noticed me crying and came over to hug me. She said, "It'll be OK. We've been doing the same thing. We had a drive for them yesterday. They were able to come in and get things and they weren't charged for them. It's sad and it really gives us something to be grateful for. Do you want to sit down for a minute and get yourself together?"

I wiped the tears from my face and smiled to assure her that I'd be fine. I whispered, "Thank you," and walked away.

By the time I made it back to them, Nissie looked up at me and said, "Now how you gone be a volunteer worker and you over there crying harder than anybody? Didn't they just tell us in that training class to not let them see us upset?"

Still collecting myself and trying to not think about it, I said, "Girl I know what they said, but that baby is without his mother and doesn't know where she is. I wasn't ready for that."

Bren looked over at me and said, "You're pitiful, you're crying harder than Trenika and Jasmine." Tina bowed her head and walked away while saying, "Now I know it's time for me to go. I can't do this."

A young lady was with a baby, picking out clothes for her. Bren walked over to her and said, "I'll get that stuff for you if you want me to."

The lady smiled and looked a little surprised, but also pleased with Bren's offer. Tina and a few of us would pitch in and buy a couple pairs of shoes to match the outfits that Bren bought and a football for the boys.

Nissie had sent them to us once she saw what they had picked out and wanted to get. After our purchases, we took the items to the parking lot where the fire department had set up shop and asked whether they could use some volunteers. We'd come back tomorrow.

The lady who took the toys initially said that we could come back tomorrow, but after a minute she said, "Y'all are already here. I'm sure we can find something for y'all to do. Go park back there and come on."

We helped sort, organize and make up the gift bags that were being given to evacuees. They also had hot food and cold drinks. They were grilling hot dogs, hamburger patties and sausage.

They had a wide selection of chips, nuts, crackers, cookies, nutrition bars, candy, gum and drinks. They weren't sure if enough people knew that they were still there, so some of us went to pass the word that they were in the same general location, only a street over.

Nissie, Tina, Smokie and I walked back up towards the Astrodome. We were going to stop everyone who we passed to let them know where they could go and get a free bite to eat.

We also had signs with the directions so one way or another, they would know about the donation site. Other people and organizations were present and standing on the corners too. They were passing out information and engaging evacuees in conversation.

Some were noticeably irritated while others were somewhat subdued and lacked emotion. For me it was a bit overwhelming and humbled my heart considerably.

All of them had a story to tell and no matter how important or insignificant, it was the only thing that was still *theirs*.

We had only planned to put in a couple of hours, but it eventually turned into about six or seven. It was hard to leave once we began to talk to them and imagine what this had to feel like.

We would also end up passing out T-shirts for a store that was giving them away to evacuees. They were grateful that we were willing to do it for them, since we would be walking the grounds and speaking with many of them. The evacuees were most grateful for what had been shown them by Houstonians. Many stated that they had never seen so much compassion and good deeds shared before. My heart smiled every time I heard this.

There were also many tears and hugs to be shared by all. An older gentleman went as far as saying that the hugs from us were the first he had since experiencing 9/11, in which his wife was a victim.

He pulled out pictures of a very beautiful and younger Asian woman. She had flowing, waist length, coal black hair.

Her smile was a mischievous one, but sweet and innocent just the same.

We stood and let him talk about her for quite some time. We didn't want to cut him off or his memory of her. After he finished, he thanked us for the hugs and listening to him tell his story. It seemed unfair that two of America's most memorable catastrophes had singled him out twice.

We soon ran into a sister who was very frustrated with things and how they were being treated by agencies that were set up to render aid to them.

She stated that she wasn't looking for anyone to "give" her anything, only that they respect and treat her decently and humanely. I was quite surprised when she told me that a Red Cross worker hung up in her face while she was talking to them.

She shared that she had gotten the opportunity to speak with a family member back home. They told her that her home had been used as a source of shelter by some of those who happened to be left in the area. Although she didn't mind their seeking shelter in it, she hoped that they wouldn't vandalize it.

There were ten of them here in Houston, with her mother still residing in a shelter in New Orleans. She was stressed to the highest order.

Her work ethic and character were evident, even in the little time that I conversed with her. She didn't care if they got a one-room apartment with one bowl, one cup and one fork and spoon. As long as they could all be together and reclaiming their shattered lives, she was all for it.

I found myself getting tickled when she'd get excited. Her voice was somewhat mellow, but it would pick up and start a rapid succession of verbiage, when she stopped and thought about how some people were treating them. Her accent almost sounded as if she were from Jamaica.

I exchanged information with her and told her that I'd be in touch with what I could find out and to assist them with anything that they might need and weren't getting quick enough. We ended it with a hug and the belief that things would get better. Her name was Bridget.

As Trenika and I ventured closer to the Astrodome, trying to see if we could get in, a lady with the type of video camera that was indicative of a media outlet was getting footage of people standing outside the doors of the center.

I asked what station she was with and she replied, "The Source. It'll be on channel 21. It's a Christian Broadcasting Station that'll be launching in September some time."

I said, "OK, be sure that you let viewers know of the challenges that face evacuees and how important it is that they receive the right information and in a timely fashion. They're frustrated that not enough is known to them."

She stepped back, started the camera and politely said, "You're on, tell the people what you want them to know." Trenika slid to the right and left me sitting there utterly dumbfounded that I was going to be on this broadcast with my hair all over my head, sweating like a convict on the run and ill-prepared to address viewers anywhere.

Nonetheless, I made the best of the situation and sent out a plea for people to come out and walk amongst the evacuees. Have information readily available for them and most of all let them know that people, as a whole, were concerned for them.

We were all quite beat by this time and we were rounding one another up to head back home. We gathered near the entrance gates and started our trek back to the donation site.

We stopped and shared information along the way, but the heat was working us over time. I had a bottle of water and it had gotten hot. I opened it up and poured it down the front of my T-shirt.

Smokie looked at me like I was losing touch and I assured her that what little wind that came along and hit the wet areas felt good. I had her to try it for herself.

When we got back to the site, they were in need of items to be sorted and packaged for evacuees that were coming up in pretty good numbers now. We went ahead and decided that we'd give them a little more time and filled orders for those coming up for aid.

Upon completion of our time there, we let them know that we'd be trying to make it back tomorrow too. It turned out to be a really nice experience.

That was time well spent and it seemed to have done us all some good. Once we got into it, it was too hard to stop. Somehow we always found an extra ounce of strength to do a tad bit more.

"I'm getting home and going straight to bed." Smokie said. Everyone seemed to be in agreement with that. The walking, heat and emotional weakening had me beat for sure.

When I did get home, there were two messages from the Katy Chamber of Commerce waiting on me. One was on the answering machine and the other was e-mail.

They needed people to go to the "Breakfast Klub," the next day (Sunday), to assist with accepting donations and sorting and bagging them.

I called Nissie to let her know that we had gotten another 'job.' I pretty much knew I'd be able to swing it since I was off on that Monday, due to it being Labor Day.

After I told her what and where we'd be doing it, she laughed lightly and said, "Shan, make sure you don't over work us too much, OK?" I laughed right along with her because this is one of the most 'volunteering everybody else's services' sister I've ever seen in my life (ask Bren, LOL). I gave her the specifics and we both dropped off to sleep.

Visions of sugarplums didn't dance in my head, but for some strange reason plastic trash bags and car trunks sure did.

I'm scaring myself now. The thought of car trunks, plastic bags and anything remotely close to death didn't belong in the same sentence.

For obvious reasons I continued to try and shake unpleasant things from my mind and replaced them with happier thoughts and ideas.

I didn't want to think of the long suffering and unnecessary reasons for the deaths of these poor people. I almost wished that my alarm clock would go off and I'd find that I was having one of the worst nightmares of my life.

That wouldn't happen and I'd keep going around in a haze, not following the news, not allowing anyone to talk to me about it and not admitting to myself that this was real and it happened right here in the great U. S. of A.

My daughters cautiously watched me and made no mention of what was going on, but they were curious to know what was going on inside of me.

Chapter Two

I got up and went to church prepared to leave there going to the Breakfast Klub. Man if you could have seen the look on the faces of some of the saints.

It was first Sunday and the looks on their faces suggested that they were wondering why I was dressed in a T-shirt and capris. As long as God knows, I guess that's all that matters.

I went to Bren and asked if she and Smokie were going to accompany us. She had no idea what I was talking about.

Nissie didn't get the opportunity to ask her about going with us, so she was not in the least bit prepared to leave church and volunteer.

We decided that on the way we'll drop by her house and allow her to change, then we'll go from there. My car had been running hot and I was a little concerned about that because I was going to be traveling rather far out and I had no idea where I'd be, in case someone had to come and get us, were it to overheat and cut off.

God's a deliverer. He let nothing happen to the car as we journeyed there. It also helped that we found where we were going fairly easily.

The Breakfast Klub is a tiny, homey restaurant that boasts all the feelings of home. It's a hot spot among some of the most influential people in Houston.

There was standing room only and it wasn't long before they had to start turning volunteers away. The donations, people and steady flow of traffic were more than bursting at the seams.

To our surprise, Congresswoman Sheila Jackson-Lee was there, handling business as only she can. She's a woman of small stature, but when she speaks her confidence and delivery project a much larger woman and persona.

Her words are direct and persuasive. I was quite impressed with the way that she attained and kept the attention of those gathered around her as she spoke.

They were community leaders, pastors of area churches, and other men on the move, vying for her attention and thoughts on their suggestions or offerings.

She shared much with them, they shared much with her and time seemed to fly. It was hot as could be and due to the already over-crowded status of the restaurant, we were outside in the blazing heat.

What little shade we had been able to hide behind slowly began to ease away from us. This was only a three-hour commitment, so it saved the day for us.

I was very impressed when a homeless man walked up and asked one of the gentlemen who was standing near her for some spare change.

Without a second thought, she turned, looking around for something to give him, but her aide reached into his pocket, pulled out a couple of bills and handed them to him.

The hour was far spent and it wasn't long before we had to start pulling the donations out of the restaurant and piling them in the parking lot so that they'd be ready to load, once the truck got there to pick them up.

The community came out in force and supported this worthy cause. We were amazed with all of the items that had been given for the evacuees.

We'd leave there and make a scheduled appearance at a skating party with one of Bren's co-workers. Tonya and crew are a lively little bunch. They're always down for a little fun.

It was hilarious to see a few of them fall. I won't share who they were, but Trenika, Smokie, Blue, and Bren know who they are. Nissie might've fallen too, had she ever left the carpet long enough.

As the night wore on, and between skating, everybody was talking about how the sun and walking of the prior days had zapped them of their strength.

While she was deciding whether or not she'd get on the floor, Nissie was sure to tell me that Labor Day was her day to rest and she didn't want to do anything other than that.

Yeah OK, I'll give her that. Siiiiiiike!

Chapter Three

I called Bridget, one of the evacuees that I had the pleasure of meeting and keeping in contact with. I wanted to see how things were going with them and she shared a few immediate needs with me. I jotted them down and told her that I'd meet her later to give them to her. She and her family were staying with friends here in Houston.

I had already decided that I wouldn't pay rent so some of their needs could be met and this would give me the perfect opportunity to go ahead and get it out of the way. Now all I had to do was see how I could get them to her.

I got in touch with Nissie to see if she'd ride over that way with me, since I'm not familiar with how to get there and she started in with that fussing.

"Didn't I tell you that today was my day and that I was going to be doing nothing but resting?" I let her get her satisfaction out and just as easily as she started, she said, "OK, that'll give me the chance to get those clothes to Sheila. I can be getting them together while you're on the way."

Sheila was one of the people we met when we were volunteering with the fire department. She had relatives from New Orleans living with her and one of them had a ten-day-old baby. We called and set up a meeting place to deliver care packages to them.

We'd get to meet two of them at one time and get another need fulfilled. It was going as smoothly as I planned.

When we got there Sheila was already waiting and that made it so much easier. Bridget had gotten a call through to FEMA and couldn't leave, so we waited a little longer and decided that we'd leave her things at the customer service desk at the Toys-R-Us store that we were at earlier in the week.

The whole trip and delivery wasn't nearly as bad as I thought it might be and we made it back in at a very decent hour.

Nissie did have other plans and although she fussed at me, she really does like helping people and will give her last. Maybe now she'll think twice about volunteering other people. Somehow I doubt that though.

She had some more things for Sheila and told her that she'd drop them off later in the week because some of the items that had been misplaced and ended up somewhere else.

"Oh girl! I forgot to tell you that I did the radio interview with Bishop Victor Curry, who is out of Florida. Remember the author I told you about, who I met when I went to Atlanta this summer?"

She sat there as if trying to recall all that I was sharing with her and finally said, "Yeah, I remember you telling me something about that. You talked to them on the radio this morning?"

I shook my head and said, "Yes ma'am, bright and early. She called and he interviewed me for about fifteen or twenty-minutes, and that was that. They were having a 'radio-thon' and will be sending needed items to help the Katrina evacuees."

"Oh girl that's nice. Did you tell them the things that they seem to need most?" she asked. I looked at her and rolled my eyes, saying, "You already know."

We just sat there in silence a minute. Taking in all that we had tried to do and all that would need to be done to help these survivors of Katrina.

I dropped her off at home and went in to prepare myself for another day of work.

Our little mission was only beginning.

Chapter Four

On my break I decided to call Bridget and she was very upset. FEMA was issuing out debit cards and it turned out to be pretty disastrous.

She said that the people were hot and standing in lines that snaked around as far as you could see. A lady fainted and it got more chaotic.

The water that was being handed out and ice packs were doing very little in this Houston heat. It was made worse when police locked the place down for a while, once evacuees became irate and started loudly voicing their concerns over the way that they were being treated.

I assured her that all would be well and that her caring spirit and knowledge of God would be the things to get them through this.

She wasn't only looking out for herself. She was sure to pass along any and all information to other evacuees and she'd even go as far as skipping on something so that one of them might be able to have. She was a volunteer/evacuee and did it without having to be poked or prodded into it.

She was missing her mother terribly, but she didn't want to take her from one shelter in one state and place her in another one in a different state.

If and when she brought her here, she wanted it to be in her own home.

When I made it in from work, I crashed immediately. It had been a very long and busy weekend for me and I was still trying to catch up with myself. It didn't even seem like there was a holiday in there (sigh).

Chapter Five

Tonight will be my first night working at the George R. Brown Convention Center and I had the nerve to sign up for a double shift. I don't know how I'm going to manage that, but I'll know by the time it's over.

I can't help but be amazed at how neat and orderly most of the evacuees seem to be, under these conditions.

As I walk, I see the vast majority of them shuffling around and straightening up their belongings.

An older gentleman is sitting and reading the newspaper, rather loudly, to himself. A woman has the phone book and is jotting down information as her children sleep.

Many of them stop me to talk and it's really quite interesting to have them share as they do. They talk about everything from pets they may have had to cracks in their sidewalks.

To someone else it might be trivial, but to them it was everything and that's the way I wanted to make them feel. If it was important to them, then it was equally as important to me.

I made notes to myself. I wanted to remember everything and everybody who I came in contact with. I wanted to forever have a memory of the impact that this had in my life and those who I would meet.

I was careful to not do it in a way that would make anyone uneasy. I didn't want them to think that I was surveying them or observing their physical being.

I was merely jotting down thoughts as they came to me and as I witnessed them.

Random Thoughts

September 10, 2005 - My first night going in as an "Operation Compassion" Volunteer. I got lost and had to rely on the directions of a very cute and 'tiny' policeman. He was one of the smallest police officers that I ever recall seeing and then when I had, it was a woman.

I watched as he pointed here and then over there, with the tattoo of his little girl being proudly displayed on the inside of his right arm. His eyes strayed for a moment, but I was too involved with trying to remember where he was sending me to put too much thought into it.

"If you get to the Toyota Center, you've gone too far. You can't miss it. It's a straight shot. If you get lost, come back here and I'll get you there." He smiled as he said this.

I studied his face a brief moment and responded, "You're getting a kick out of this aren't you? You like knowing that I'm a damsel in distress and need you to help me out. Nothing like a woman who doesn't know her way around, huh?"

He let out an impressive little chuckle and said, "Naw, I don't mean to make it seem like that. You're just so serious looking and stuff, it's not that bad really and I'll make sure that you get there, OK?"

I sighed and purred, "Yeah, but if I can't get *there*, pray tell how I'd be able to make it back *here* to ask your help again?" He assured me that his directions were dead on the money and there would be no way that I'd get lost. He was right.

I smiled to myself as everything that he said I'd see and pass, came into view. I found the designated parking lot and made my way into the building, with an escort who was seeing volunteers in and out of the center.

I was working the 10:00 p.m. to 10:00 a.m. shift and I didn't have the slightest idea what to expect, but I do know that I didn't want to be haplessly wandering around the parking lot. We had already been trained that we should travel in groups, for the sake of safety.

This was not because of the evacuees that were in the area either. It was for basic safety precautions, period. Crime was going on before they arrived and it wasn't going to go on vacation because they were here, but I'd bet that the slightest rise in it would be blamed on them just the same.

The first group of people whom I'd meet would be a group of teens who were sitting around teasing one another and making a 'mild ruckus.'

Lena, Brittney, Mya, Marvin, Melvin and Ron were taking one another's trinkets and other small 'busy items' that had been given to them by organizations at the shelter.

Lena was the 'mother' acting one in the group. She seemed to have a wonderful time issuing orders and keeping them in line.

Marvin had taken a ball from her and she was in the process of trying to retrieve it from him when I walked over.

"Hey now, what's up with y'all?" They looked rather doe-eyed at one another, as if contemplating who would speak first.

It would be Lena. "He took my ball from me and won't give it back." She pointed towards Marvin and he grinned sheepishly and said, "Uhn uhnnn…She told me I could see it and now she wants it back."

I looked over at her, she pursed her lips and said, "I let him see it about an hour ago, but now he won't give it back."

I scanned the faces of the others there. The two girls were nodding their heads and the two boys were displaying poker faces.

I pretty much gathered that she was not lying. I turned to him and said, "Marvin, come on now. I came over here because I saw that cute little smile of yours and thought you were a sweet kind of fella. You mean to tell me that you are teasing her like this?"

What I say that for? He started blushing and still put up a good front. "For real, she did say that I could have it. You can ask them." When I followed his pointing finger towards Ron and Melvin, they looked like they weren't even trying to hear him.

"Ummm...Marvin, why is it that I get the feeling that they juuuust don't see it your way?" They all started laughing and started in again with the accusations and differences of opinion.

I made one final appeal for him to be a 'good guy' and return the ball to her and he did. She then sent me over to talk to her mother "Aunt T" and her little brother, Joshua, who was two.

Her mother, who sat at a table across from them, seemed to have gotten a thrill from monitoring them and their teen-aged camaraderie. She obviously allowed them a little space, but she kept a watchful eye on them. I didn't disturb her too much, she was on her cell phone and I wanted to be as less intrusive as possible.

I then met Jerry, a native Texan who was beaming that he had gotten a job just this day. He grinned that he'd be working at a furniture company making $8.80 an hour.

"I'll be able to move into my apartment tomorrow and with having the job, I'll be starting off pretty good. Don't you think?" he asked.

I smacked my lips and said, "Honey, if that ain't real good, I don't know what is. You're starting off with a salary better than minimum wage and an apartment."

The smile returned to his face. He had a beautiful set of off white teeth. Then out of nowhere I hear, "Hey Shandra! Glad to see one of *us* up in here! We're glad *they're* helping us, but *they* don't know."

A gentleman who was on his way back down to the sleeping area, located on the lower level of the George R. Brown Convention Center, shouted this as he was leaving from having a late night snack.

I was a bit dumbfounded by his statement, but Jerry went on to explain that disaster volunteers had pretty much been white and I would hear those sentiments repeated several times throughout the night.

I met Celestine and Ella, two sisters who made it down with their children. Ella has nine and Celestine has two daughters. They were venting their frustrations at having nowhere to be and the fact that Ella's son needed to be in a more private and centralized location.

Celestine spoke of how both of her daughters were able to make it to two different states safely and the son of one of them did not want to leave with his mother because he was raised by Celestine and was not about to leave her side.

They wanted housing and they wanted to know that all was going to be well. They didn't want to be in 'bad neighborhoods' because they wanted something different for their children.

They spoke freely of the crime, corruption, misery and hopelessness that seemed to have a hold on all of them. Ella spoke of how they no longer reacted to gunfire or news of horrendous crimes. Desensitization is what best describes what they had become accustomed to.

Although sometimes fearful of what might befall them, they shared that they've never been able to give up hope that God would see them through whatever circumstance presented itself to them.

In fact, they believe that through 'divine intervention,' NOLA, as some fondly refer to New Orleans, has been made to see the error of her wicked ways.

Mardi Gras had been the mainstay for this mystifying city and it pumped much money into the economy, but the under side of it has been kept hush-hush.

During Mardi Gras, New Orleans is a festive city with half-naked women who swing in and out of the windows of businesses on Bourbon Street. Some of them go as far as flashing augmented breasts to rebel-rousers, which leaves little room to wonder why many would prefer to remember and embrace this as opposed to a seventy-five percent unemployment rate, larger scale crime rate, rampant illiteracy, and a leadership of uncertainty.

They were fairly happy with the services of the Red Cross and other agencies that had taken up residence in the GRBCC, but the sooner they could get into their own place to call home and begin to rebuild, the better.

I asked them what they thought of the people who were somewhat critical of evacuees who did not care to be on the cruise ships that FEMA had secured to house them, while docked at Galveston.

The look on their faces changed and simultaneously they agreed that, "*They* weren't there. *They* could never know what we felt, what we saw, how *that* water changed everything for us, nor what it is to be here now with people who don't seem to care about us or want us here and then ask us to go and live surrounded by water? It's been hard for me even taking showers after that."

I felt the lump in my throat and knew that it was my signal to leave before the crying began. I reached out and touched both of their hands and asked if I could give them a hug. They were too happy for me to and I moved on.

I continued on my way and had one of the residents to stop me and ask, "Lawd! They couldn't get any other colored shirts than that bright yellow?" Being quick on my feet, I replied, "It's gold and it is meant to remind us of the 'Golden

Rule.' 'Do unto others as you would have them do unto you.'"

On the front were the words "Operation Compassion" and on the back "Hurricane Katrina Relief Team."

I could tell that it all made sense to her then. I winked and kinda smiled at the fact that I had been able to respond with something as fitting.

As I went up and down the aisles in the three different sections of the GRBCC, I couldn't help but recall the number of people, "Eric," one of the Team Leaders, said had been fed for lunch and dinner earlier that day.

He stated that at lunch there were about 10,000 who had been fed and at dinner about 8,000. I don't know where those numbers came from and it was too hard for me to even begin to calculate, but this was still during the early stages of getting the evacuees situated, so it's definitely feasible.

He further stated that if we should be working downstairs in the sleeping quarters that we should not harass them, but make them comfortable and be understanding of their plight and validate their fears, confusion and anxieties.

He said that many of them just want to talk and share their experience and know that someone cares. He went on to say that we could pray with them, if they wanted us to, but that we should not 'force' it on them.

What I saw next was interesting, to say the least. A young evacuee, about ten years old, was walking back and forth through a group of the relief workers, running his hands through their hair, as if taking a survey of its softness or comfort appeal.

Most of them smiled at him and did not seem to be offended with this display of affection. One or two were more surprised by it, but none of them made a big deal out of it.

At 11:00 p.m. was 'lights out' and we were instructed to try and urge the residents to be quieting down and mindful that many would be sleeping during this time.

Mary, who was very cheerful and down to earth was observing and making mental notes, just as I was. I could tell by the deep looks and expressions as we passed through the aisles.

Every now and again one of us would openly exclaim, "I can't even imagine." Looking at the packed conditions, lack of real privacy and scattered existence, was just too over-whelming.

It was a little city. There was an impromptu hair salon, barbershop, ironing station, movie-theater, some had personalized DVD players and were kind enough to share them with other sleepless residents.

The GRB had many services active and on site, which added to the feel of an organized community. There was a Chapel, the WIC office, a post office, medical triage, transportation, Red Cross, FEMA, vision screening, a cell phone charging table, a computer station, and a phone center where evacuees could keep in touch with loved ones.

Showers and laundry were located in the back of the quarters. Along with regular restrooms, there were also portable toilets to the rear of the facility.

Hand sanitizing tables were located *everywhere*. That was right on time for me. I am a 'germaphobe' and needed to have access to them accordingly.

Mary and I laughed when we saw an older gentleman snuggling up with a teddy bear. He looked up and saw us looking at him and gave us an embarrassed smile. We assured him that we'd keep that to ourselves and we did. If that was all he needed to help him feel comfortable, who were we to say otherwise?

Nearly two rows over we observed a very talkative and wide-awake six-year-old. He had a car sliding it back and forth in front of him, as he was talking to a gentleman who appeared to be his father.

His 'father' looked at him lovingly and never lifted his eyes from him. As we passed them, we noticed the tears streaming down his face.

We were glad when Chuck came along. He was a hard man who barked out very precise and distinct orders. He had a 'no nonsense' kind of attitude.

Seeming arrogant at first, that soon faded after a little while of working with him. One could get the feel that he was very serious about his job and what he wanted those on his watch to do.

As the adult residents continued to talk on their cell phones or read, the children roller-skated, jumped rope or played cards.

Mary and I had been laughing at something that one of us shared when we heard an older gentleman shout, "Y'all better get ya' asses over there with that ball. If ya' hit me I'm gone beat 'cha little asses and I mean that!"

We looked at one another as if getting confirmation that we should step in and try to contain the situation. We went over and repositioned the boys so that they'd be farther away from residents who were trying to sleep.

We also reminded them that it would soon be time for them to settle in for the night. They weren't too happy to hear that, but it was expected and we would do whatever necessary to enforce it. She walked over and chatted with a little old lady and I slowly trudged on, giving her enough time to catch up with me when she finished.

Chuck came over and pulled us to do a head count. We were positioned across the floor and had to stop everyone who passed us, to get ID numbers.

Some were familiar with the process, while others wanted to know "Why do you need this?" We eagerly explained that it was to try and keep a pretty accurate account of who was there and how many where there.

One gentleman was walking towards us when I stepped up to ask him for his and he quickly asked, "Hey, you wanna dance?"

"Why sure!" I chimed in. We embraced, pressed our cheeks together and I very appropriately hummed a nice little tune to set the mood.

After we were done he bowed and walked away. Everyone was in complete laughter by then. The residents had been in very good spirits and seemed to give *us* a reason to smile and be grateful for the experience of working with and for them.

With about seven of us taking the head count, it wasn't long before it was over and we were back pacing the floors and ready to assist anyone who might need it.

"Where's the rest of us? We ain't seen but one or two black people here?" When I swung around to see who had voiced that, an older gentleman was sitting on the edge of his air mattress, checking me out and taking inventory it seemed.

He looked at me from head to toe and then repositioned himself to be able to get a closer look at the gold cross that I wear around my neck.

I smiled at him and said, "They'll be here. We'll be out in shifts and people are choosing shifts that work best for them and other obligations."

"Oh, OK I was just wondering. We gotta stick together and when we didn't see more of *us* out here…" I interrupted him because this was the $64,000 question, for this night anyway, and I wanted to get through with it.

"Naw, we family. Ain't nobody gone bail on you now," I said. He smiled a big empty grin, two of his front teeth missing.

I let out a long, deep sigh and glance over at the clock, it's 2:00 a.m. and I have quite a few more hours to go. I'm pulling a 10 p.m. – 10 a.m. and time is not on my side.

During one of our rotations we noticed about four young men who were glued to a DVD player. I asked, "Y'all can't sleep either, huh?" The one who appeared to be the owner of it said, "Naw, we got a good movie going. Wanna watch it with us?"

I smiled and inquired, "What's the name of it?" A broad and devious smile came over his face when he replied, "Jason Goes To Hell."

I declined on the movie, but somehow a trip to hell seemed to be something that Hurricane Katrina evacuees could identify with.

Tina, one of the other volunteers, came over and asked us whether we had the opportunity to visit the "Kids Zone," which had been set up for the children.

Mary and I explained that we hadn't and she went on to tell us how much fun she had experienced while working the earlier shift.

She was talking about how wild and crazy it got with the games and interaction between staff and the children and urged us to consider coming in early enough one night to see it for ourselves. We told her we'd consider it.

The cleaning crew was making its rounds since most were in bed and out of the way. They'd sweep down one long end and leave a pile of trash and then go down the other, doing the same thing.

One stopped when he came across a boxed puzzle that was lying on the floor with a big gaping hole in the bottom of the box. Carefully designed pieces strewn about its container having a huge hole…Louisiana no doubt.

Even in their sleep, many of the evacuees seemed restless. I watched as the expressions on their faces changed and how they seemed to struggle or reach out for something that wasn't there and then settle back down.

Men folk stayed up keeping a watchful eye over their families and loved ones. Every now and again you might catch one of them dozing, but for the most part he was sitting up in a chair, arms folded across his chest and daring anything to come along and threaten their existence *again*.

My phone started beeping again. My battery was low and I needed to get it charged up. I walked over to the re-charging station and signed it in. Whoever came up with the idea of making this a necessary station is rather clever. Many of the residents had cell phones and not having to worry about keeping the battery charged and ready to go had to have been a relief.

No sooner than I checked it in, I was suddenly made aware of a tiny body making its way to the back of the center. It was somewhat dark and I couldn't quite make out whether it was a male or female.

Nonetheless, I figured that they were going to the restroom, so I paid full attention to them and headed in the direction that they were going.

As I got closer I realized that it was a little girl of about eight. I observed as she went into the restroom and told Mary that I had no intentions of leaving until she was out. When she wasn't out in a few minutes I went in to see what might be taking her so long and found her playing in the soap and water.

I didn't say anything to her, with my mouth that is, but I shot her a playful "you know better than that" look and kindly followed her back to her sleeping quarters.

I don't want to make it seem like anyone there was 'criminal,' but I wasn't too keen on her walking around this great big place alone. Especially with it being dark and not as many eyes and ears being open for whatever.

If anything was going to happen to her, it wouldn't be on my watch. I don't know how true reports were from the Superdome or any of the other places that initially housed evacuees, but let the record clearly and presently show that hell would have rained on somebody *this* night, had any harm come to this baby.

I'm not the "baddest" person in the world, but when it comes to children and 'seasoned people' I'm a force to be reckoned with.

We were pulled from walking and monitoring and asked to go by and do a bed check. We'd have to look for beds that looked as if there were no occupants and break them down.

This was fairly easy and we could use a change of duty. Just walking was getting kinda boring and we wanted something else.

After about ten minutes of this a young man came over to us and asked, "Can one of y'all talk to her?" He pointed in the direction of a young lady, who seemed to be distraught.

She was a pretty girl who looked to be in her mid to late twenties. Her hair was in shambles and she walked without purpose and glanced around sharply, thoroughly, as if looking for someone.

She had on a pair of jeans and an ill-fitting blouse. She started to walk one way and then as if by second thought abruptly turned and went another.

I looked quizzically at Mary and back to him stating, "We're in the middle of something, but as soon as we're done and if she wants to talk, we'd be more than happy to help her out."

He looked over at her again and then back at us, "OK, but she really needs to talk to somebody. She's losing it."

By the time Mary and I finished pulling unused cots, we couldn't find the young lady who was in need of a friend. We decided to go upstairs and get a drink.

When we were on our way down, we saw her sitting at the table with all of the phones. "Mary look! There she is. You want to see if she wants to talk?" I asked.

Mary didn't miss a beat and said, "Yes, she probably just needs someone to listen to her and make her feel that she's not alone in how she feels."

We slowly approached her and as I got closer, I lay my hands on her shoulder. "Are you OK, Sweetie?" I asked.

By this time the tears were non-stop. She shook her head and got off of the phone with whomever it was she was talking to.

"No, I'm not OK. They can't find my three year-old," she said through broken sobs. I looked over at Mary and we both seemed to have felt the impact of that statement.

"Who can't find your baby?" I asked. She was shaking violently and continued to try and talk through the tears.

"My sister had her with her at the Superdome, but somehow they got separated and she can't find my baby. She has my one year old, but she lost the older one and I don't know what I'll do without my baby."

She broke down again and by this time I was no better. I didn't even want to imagine what she was going through. I began to rub her back and urged her to try and not let it beat her down too much because she still needed her strength.

"I haven't eaten or slept in five days. I can't do anything but think about them and how they got separated. I never let my babies out of my sight. They were always with me and now one of them is somewhere and I can't find her."

"Sweetie, what is your name? What is your baby's name? I'm Shandra and this is Mary." She slowed down from crying long enough to tell us that her name was Tijuana and her daughter's name is Hope. The one who is accounted for is named D'Yasia.

"OK, Tijuana, do you think you can go upstairs and grab something to eat? You need your strength and we'd hate for you to get yourself sick and not be able to take care of the babies when they do get here."

It took her a minute to respond, but when she did, it seemed a lost cause. "I'm not hungry. I want my babies. That's all I care about right now." She lay her head back on the table and cried some more.

I looked over at Mary and she basically shrugged her shoulders as if she didn't know what else we could do. Coming out of nowhere I asked, "Can I pray for you, Tijuana?"

She lifted her head and said, "Yes ma'am. I always pray."

"Father I come to you tonight asking that you bring peace of mind to this mother in her darkest hour. Lord I ask that you give her back her joy and reason to believe. Father I further ask that wherever Hope may be, that You'll keep your loving arms around her and keep her safe from all things seen and unseen. Let someone find her and bring her where she needs to be. Let them not rest until they know that they've done all they could to reunite this mother and daughter. Lord, You sit high and look low. You KNOW all that we can only imagine and for that we will stand on your word and know that Hope is going to be OK and brought home soon. Father, give her strength to deal with whatever your will prescribes. Bring back her appetite and desire to sleep. Father bless all who have suffered through this and those who have found it in their hearts to be of service to these, your people. All this I ask in your son Jesus' name, thank God...Amen."

After the prayer she started to talk a little about herself and the girls and was sure to mention how 'good' a mother she was.

That indicated to me that she was feeling some sort of guilt over the way things had happened and she needed to know that others did not think badly of her because of it.

Mary touched her arm and said, "Hon, you're cold. Can I get you a blanket?" Tijuana nodded and Mary was off to find one for her.

I took down all of their names and was sure to let her know that I'd be asking believers to pray for them. She was somewhat settled, but if too much time lapsed between our speaking, she'd drift off and start thinking about Hope again.

"Tijuana, your baby's name is all the reason you need to believe that she's going to be OK. Her name is Hope, what better name to have in a time like this? I want you to concentrate on getting better for D'Yasia and doing what you can for her. If you are weak and worn from worrying about Hope, you have another child who'll miss out on you. Do you understand that?" I asked.

She looked at me and as I looked into her eyes, I could feel her pain. I could tap into every damning thing about not knowing where your child is or whether or not they are dead or alive.

"I'm trying to be strong, really I am, but I don't know how my sister could leave her alone like that." She put her head in her hands and began to cry again.

"Tijuana, look at me Sweetie." She slowly lifted her head and said, "Ma'am?" I smiled and brushed a strand of hair from her face. "Please don't blame your sister for this, you don't have all of the facts yet and you have to know that she is hurting too. Don't you know that this has got to be eating her to the core to know that she was responsible for your baby and somehow lost her? Don't turn this into a time of anger and unhappiness with your sister. Is Hope a wanderer? Could she have wandered off while your sister was asleep?"

She immediately shook her head and said, "No, Hope wouldn't have done that. She knows about strangers and wouldn't have left my sister's side."

I bowed my head and asked God to give me something to give to her, something that would help. Everything else seemed to be drawing a blank.

"Tijuana, what if she went looking for you? What if she realized that you weren't there and she went looking for you? Would she have gotten up and walked away then?"

I felt bad when she burst out crying again, but it was worth it once she said, "Yes, she would have gotten up to look for me. I can't blame my sister for that. I just didn't know how it could happen, but now I can understand."

Mary took her hand and guided Tijuana's head down to the table and said, "We'll be here a bit longer. You go ahead and get some sleep. Shhh…shhh…shhh…it's OK."

Tijuana laid her head on the table. Mary and I pulled the covers up to her neck and as one hummed, the other rubbed her back and in no time she was fast asleep.

Mary and I sat and watched over her like any protective mother would. Every now and again we'd steal a glance at one another and shake our heads. We were careful not to say anything that might upset her, were she to overhear us.

We were able to watch over her for nearly an hour. She slowly began to stir and said that she had a bad headache. I told her that it was more than likely a hunger headache and that she should put something light on her stomach and take something for the headache.

She was adamant that she couldn't eat, but after I convinced her that the headache would only linger and possibly get worse, she went with me upstairs to get a bite to eat.

I was showing her the crackers, donuts, fruit, cereal bars, etc. None of it appealed to her, but she picked up an apple anyway.

We walked and surveyed the place a little. She talked more and seemed to be in better spirits. She began to eat the apple and that was violently interrupted when she began to gag on it.

I pointed her to a trashcan and told her to stand over it until she was sure that she wasn't actually going to throw up. After a few tense minutes of that we headed back downstairs.

We went to her cot and she put her things in a little bucket near her bed. She had nothing. She made it out in only the clothes she had on and someone gave her the little pink purse that she was carrying.

I had her to crawl up in bed and lie there, even if she thought she couldn't get any sleep. We were instructed that we could talk to and visit with residents, but I didn't want anyone to believe that I was spending too much time with her and neglecting the duties that I was there to do.

After she settled in and dozed off I went on about my rounds. By this time Mary would be leaving soon and I'd be getting after it by myself, unless I found someone else to partner up with.

Mary and I exchanged information since we found that we were in the same part of town. We might even ride in with one another on one of the future nights. That would work out fine. She asked to be made aware of everything that we could find out about the baby and updates on all of them.

When she saw the 4:00 a.m. to 10:00 a.m. shift coming, she got up and waved good-bye. I pretty much had done all of the "hard" labor that I intended to, so I kinda made myself scarce and filled in where I wanted to.

I was pulling a double and I believed that gave me carte blanche to do a little something different. There were a few lazy rascals on this shift. I won't dare go into graphic details, but I definitely had to tell one, "You can't get much done with your hands in your pockets."

Man was I through when he replied, "Oh, I'm doing much, I'm thinking." Please know that a sister politely responded, "OK, I'm doing something too, I'm leaving." I clicked my heels ten times and was gone.

It bothers me when people sit back and watch everyone else do the real work, but will be the first in line to accept praise for this same work.

I've never been one to worry about praise because it's sometimes lopsided in the way that it comes to you, but a little show of appreciation is good for anyone, every now and again.

Believe it or not, my time flew by and I was sure to go by and see Tijuana before I left. She seemed sad that I was leaving and upon my assuring her that I'd be back in a couple more days, she was OK.

I gave her my phone number to reach me at and let her know that she could call at any time. When I walked out into the bright sunshine and passed the mile long line of volunteers waiting to get in, I breathed in deeply and let it out slowly.

I managed to pull it off under the most heart wrenching of circumstances and didn't get too overwhelmed by it. I was proud of myself and knew that I was reaching a new plateau in my life.

This was good for me because I needed this strength, this reassurance, and these reasons to continue to believe.

Especially since mankind had given me many reasons not to.

Chapter Six

While I was on my break today, I got a call from Bridget. She didn't want anything in particular. Just wanted me to know that they were OK and as soon as they could they would be trying to find out what was going on with their home.

She stated that I was on her mind a lot and she was grateful for all that I had done for them, and how it kept them believing in people and the goodness of God.

I assured her that what I did was not to receive any type of praise or recognition, only to know that they were all going to be OK and made to feel important no matter where they were or the circumstances.

She did mention that she has had a minute to step back and take a deep breath and focus more on that which deserves her attention, rather than the things that seemed to upset or frustrate her at first.

She's certain that things will be OK now and won't allow herself to be sidetracked by anything that isn't worthy of her positive thoughts and actions.

She assured me that she'd call once they made it back in from Louisiana. I pray that there's more there to be salvaged than written off.

They really do deserve an even break. For them to be so young and sincere in their efforts to be successful, it only seems fair that they be given as much an opportunity as possible.

"Truth be told," I can't see how she and Keith wouldn't make it, they are very strong and seem to pull their strength from each other.

Chapter Seven

I couldn't wait to get in and find Tijuana to see what was going on with her and the babies. When I last spoke to her they (an independent pilot) were going to fly her to pick up her younger baby and bring her back to the George R. Brown Convention Center with her.

This was wonderful news even though the exact whereabouts of Hope were still unknown. It was my deepest desire for her to concentrate on the one that she did have and wait until she got official word about anything else with Hope.

I walked every square inch of the center, but I didn't catch a glimpse of her anywhere. It finally dawned on me to have her paged. There was no response and I still waited in case she was upstairs or in the rest room.

I walked over to the area where they make pages from and stood for a while. I heard a lady telling one of the gentlemen at that booth that she had been hospitalized.

My heart hit the floor. I just knew that she stopped eating and sleeping and her body shut down on her. I went over to the lady and said, "I'm sorry, I really don't know how to say what I need to say, but please bear with me. I'm looking for Tijuana and I thought I heard you say that she has been hospitalized. Can you confirm that for me? I wanted to know because I was going to take her and the baby home with me, but when I got in tonight, she wasn't here and I had her paged."

Although she hadn't said anything, the look on her face let me know that something wasn't right. It turned out that Tijuana was allowing herself to be too worked up about it, without eating or sleeping and it did cause her to get sick and need a doctor's attention.

I was elated to learn that they had also found her daughter who was missing. From what I understand, Hope did get up and wander away from the sleeping sister.

A neighbor recognized her, assumed she was without her mother and kept her with her. I was tingling all over when I heard that. I couldn't be touched and I knew that God had heard and answered our prayers.

Tijuana would have to get well now and be there for the babies. I'm sure that as soon as she gets her strength up and has had the opportunity to regain her peace of mind, she'll be able to enjoy them like she has always hoped to.

She was going to be getting back to the center in a couple of hours, so I was sure to have them ask her to call me so that I could go wherever she was to see her and continue to give her encouraging words.

Nissie, Bren and Smokie came in on the 4:00 a.m. shift. I was there ready and waiting. I knew time would fly once I got with them and started acting up a little.

I went up and saw them being briefed for their shift and waited for one of them to look my way so that I could show them where the real fun was…anywhere that I might be. ~ Smile ~

I showed them the different areas and services that were being offered on site. I introduced them to people who I had met in my prior nights of service and we basically tried to keep busy.

Many residents had found housing and it was our task to break down air mattresses and sanitize them.

I had run into Celestine and Ella again, earlier. They were asking about some apartments that they would be able to move into if they saw them and liked them.

I wasn't of much help to them because I have never ventured out to that part of town and couldn't honestly say whether or not it was 'good' or 'bad.'

I told them to ask some of the other volunteers or people at the information desk. They wanted to be out of the center, but not at the risk of putting themselves or their children in harm's way.

However, after Bren and Nissie arrived, I referred them to the sisters because they are very well traveled in Houston and would have a better opinion of the areas they were mentioning.

After they shared what they knew, we went ahead and did some more walking and was caught off guard by a woman who was walking up to and cursing out some children who supposedly had been in an altercation with her children. She was daring them to even look at her children after tonight. I shook my head and we continued on, being sure that she kept legal distance from them.

She was getting a little more irritated with each statement she made, but had she gotten too close I would have intervened on the situation.

Tempers were high and tolerance was low. I can understand how it could be so, but I hoped that they would understand why it was that way and be more mindful of it when trying situations came about.

I'm glad that the children let her rant and rave and continued to walk away rather than go word for word with her and make it much worse.

This would not be the case with another family. We were assisting residents to and from the showers, pulling used beds and making a general sweep of the place when loud voices caught our attention.

We looked up and saw volunteers assisting a resident who looked to be packing up to leave, but she was embroiled in a heated exchange of words with a gentleman who two other women were trying to hold back.

Volunteers looked terrified and continued to assist her, but each time I saw them take a step or two away from her, I knew that they weren't able to handle it.

I looked over at Bren and Nissie and told them that we should probably go over and try to squash the situation. Smokie was breaking down a bed and wasn't readily available, so before things got too out of hand, I went on over and stepped up to the lady who was involved in the incident.

I got close to her and whispered, "Hey sister, come on now. We can do better than this. Let's not do this right here, right now."

She was still upset, but she responded without it being geared towards me. "I know. I'm not trying to make a scene or anything, but he came up in my face about something that isn't even his business. I had a conversation with his mother and she shared it with him and he ran up on me talking about what he'd do to me and that was when it got out of hand," she said.

The young man was still flailing about and being pulled and pushed in directions away from her, but not one minute did she flinch or show fear. She stood her ground and wanted him to know that she had no intentions of running from him.

By this time someone had gone and gotten security and they told her that they needed to get it under control. She very calmly replied that she was fine and that it was he who was making a spectacle of himself.

Another lady walked up and she told her, "You can go ahead and finish packing. I'm OK. I'm not worried about him. Get your things and let's be ready to go when all of our things are situated."

She introduced herself to me and then turned and made sure that I knew that the lady who had just walked up was her sister, as was the lady whose son was trying to get at her.

It appears that Rosetta* and Norene* felt that their sister only had time for them when it was convenient and she seemed to act differently towards them when other people were around.

This was shared with her and for some reason she told this to her son and he obviously felt the need to defend his mother's honor, thus the confrontation with his aunt.

Norene* explained that her sister was having feelings of guilt because when their mother had taken ill several years back, she was the only one of all the siblings who didn't pitch in and share the load with the rest of them.

She stated that a man or her personal life was always more important and she did what she wanted to, with little to no regards to their mother.

Sadly, their mother was one of the casualties of Katrina and that loss, along with their not being able to see or hold a proper funeral for her, had them dealing with all levels of mixed emotions.

It really broke my heart to hear this because now was a time when they surely could have been mending that fence, but after this scene, it might take a little more doing. It helped that her housing went through and she was going to be sharing an apartment with Rosetta*. They'd be away from it all real soon and could try and put it behind them.

She was nearly through with her packing when three police officers started walking back towards us. The nephew's girlfriend walked over and said, "Oh so you called the police?"

Norene* looked at her and replied, "I sure did and *this* is none of *your* business either. So please stay in your place. You're not even *in* the family."

This seemed to do it for the girlfriend, she spat out, "Oh so I'm *not* in the family huh? Since when, am I not a part of it? I've only been here for several years now!" She was making the situation worse so I grabbed her by the arm and walked her away from Norene* saying, "OK, these police officers will have no problem escorting y'all up outta here with this. Get a grip and let this mess ride. This is not the time nor place for it. Think about your baby and her seeing this. It's not a good situation either way you look at it."

She started crying and said, "I'm so sick of this shit! She makes me sick with all of this damn drama all of the time!"

I put my hand up, as if to quiet her and stated, "I'm not here to determine who's right or who's wrong, I'm trying to help y'all keep the situation under control so that none of you have different accommodations after all is said and done. Emotions are high, there's a lot going on and it doesn't take much, but you have to do your part in keeping the peace too. Can you do that?"

She looked over at Norene* and said, "Yeah, I'm gone leave her ass alone. *That's* how I'll help keep the peace." I thanked her for trying and went back over to see if Norene* was about finished with her packing.

The police officers were on their way back over to her too and that would give me the opportunity to hear what they had to say.

There was a female officer who did the talking, "OK, this is what the deal is, we went over and told him that whatever you discuss with his mother, your sister, is not any of his business, especially for him to come and make threats to you. We told him that he'd need to contain himself or we'd help him to do it. We spoke with the mom and basically told her that sisters will be sisters and what they share should remain between them without dragging their children into it. You do have grounds to go forth with charges, for his threatening you and if that's what you want to do we can assist you with it."

Norene* sat there for a moment as if unsure how to proceed with it, I took the time to bid them farewell and didn't hang around to hear what her answer might be. I wanted to make that the unknown.

However, some time after she and the one sister left, I did see the other sister (who caused the confusion), walking through the area where they had slept, crying and blankly staring at the spot where just the night before, they were all together and obviously a family.

I felt eyes on me as I passed on one of the aisles. When I turned to find them, there was a gentleman sitting up on his bed, looking at me.

He had on a hooded sweatshirt, with the hood pulled over his head. It was cold in here, but not *that* cold. I went over to him and said, "Hey now. What's going on?

He sheepishly smiled and said, "Ain't nuthin' miss, How you doing?" I smiled and replied, "I'm doing great. I've about completed a twelve and it's all good."

He pondered and then asked, "Why you here? How come you ain't at home sleep or chillin' somewhere else?"

I feigned surprise at his question. We both laughed and then I said, "Y'all are my people. This is where I'm supposed to be. If y'all suffer, I do too. When y'all soar, I will too and we all get there together. Now I got a question for you...Why aren't you asleep?"

He let out a cute little chuckle and said, "I can't sleep. There's too much to remember, too much to write and I'm trying to get it all down on paper. I want to write a book about it."

He went on to tell of how barbaric conditions were when he was over at Reliant. He said there was no order or control and that it was basically a lawless city. He went on to share many things that he witnessed, but I won't share those here as trying to substantiate or clarify would take an act of Congress.

He talked of the differences in the two places, too. The GRBCC was a lot more organized and had all kinds of stations set up and ready to assist the people with.

In his opinion the Reliant was housing the bad elements along with the good or innocent.

He even mentioned that at the GRBCC they were running closer checks on who was being allowed in. He said he was basically going to be out of luck receiving any type of aid because he originally went to New Orleans for a job when Katrina hit. He didn't live there and lost nothing, so he'll get nothing. It still seemed unfair.

We ended our conversation after his telling me the *real* reason that he was unable to sleep. "Miss, there's another reason why I can't sleep. Every time I close my eyes I keep seeing the bodies. I see 'em lying there, some with their eyes open, some with them closed. Men, women, babies…just laying out there like garbage. I can't shake it from my head and I need to."

I swallowed hard, hoping that I could say what I needed to say without cracking. "All that means is that you have to get it out of your head and put it down on paper. *You* have to tell your story. No one can share it any better than you can. Get your paper and pen and write until you can't write anymore and then you find yourself a publisher and let me see you on the 'Best Selling Author' list. I believe you can do it."

He smiled the hardest after I said this and asked me my name. "My name is Shandra…Shandra Love and who might you be?" I asked.

He extended his hand and said, "I'm Terrance, nice to meet you Shandra." I grasped his hand and said, "The pleasure was all mine. I'll see ya' next time." I winked and quickly walked away. The tears came again.

I went to get a drink and met Thomasene and Cly. They were sisters who had decided that they'd come in a little early and get the feel of things.

They were curious to know what was being shared, how the evacuees seemed to be adjusting and whether aid would be quick enough for them.

They kept me laughing a good part of the morning because they played off of one another very well. They told on one another and covered just the same in others.

You could tell that they were a handful as they came up. With all of the sister teams that I seemed to be meeting, it only made me remember how things were with my little sister and me.

They had been assigned to the shower area. I didn't particularly care to be on that specific post, but as we were walking back there and checking out the view, there were some volunteers who wanted to go and take a quick break.

They were hoping that we'd relieve them. I didn't get to open my mouth before Thomasene said, "Yeah, we'll cover while y'all break. Shandra will take care of issuing out the towels and we'll issue out the personal hygiene kits."

Then she had the nerve to look over at me and say, "Girl, I told you we weren't letting you slip away from us so easy. You gone hang with us and if I catch you trying to slip off I'll call your name out loud. You better ask Cly won't I do it."

I looked over at Cly and all she did was shake her head. I believe I just found out who the 'hell-raiser' was in their family.

We did have fun though. The women were in very talkative moods and one was kind enough to share all kinds of little secrets and anecdotes with us about cleanliness and where to put oil fragrances and perfumes.

Thomasene and I were about to die. I couldn't keep a straight face for anything and Cly was being messy. She'd keep asking the sister to repeat what she had said.

I was so glad when it got a little busy and called for me to be at my towel post a little more. I'd look at Thomasene and we'd crack up laughing all over again.

I just knew we were going to be asked not to come back. Especially when she shared that Irish Springs and Coast are not the best kind of soaps to wash your private area with.

She said that she had made the mistake of doing it and had to sit on ice packs because it tore her bottom up something fierce and had her raw down there for days.

I could sympathize with her, but had it not happened to me before I don't know that it would have seemed as funny. It felt good knowing that someone else knew firsthand what that was like.

Before long, we began to hear them call many of the residents' names over the loud speaker. That was good news in most instances. More times than not, it meant that they had secured housing for them.

I was hoping that Tijuana would find somewhere soon, even though I had already made it up in my mind that I'd let her and the girls come and stay with me.

She started stirring and I went and helped her find a change of clothes for when she was out of the shower. I was going to be leaving in a little bit and wanted to spend as much time with her as possible.

She was looking a lot better after having had a full night's rest and peace of mind in knowing that her daughters were back together and doing fine.

They came on and made the announcement that Housing and FEMA were no longer going to be available at the site after today.

They were in the process of vacating the GRBCC and eliminating programs a little at a time was in order.

Work Source, school registration, the eye clinic and banking services would be done away with as of 1:00 p.m. that day.

Although I was scheduled for two more twelve hour shifts, for the coming week, "Operation Compassion" would no longer be needed at the center because they were going to be moving everyone from that location.

With this being the case, my contact with Tijuana would be by phone until she was able to get somewhere to live.

It was a blessing that on the last day of their doors being open, she would obtain housing and did not have to worry about being shuffled to another shelter.

She was happy that the time had come for her to get on with the business of stabilizing her family and making a fresh new start, right here in Houston.

Chapter Eight

"Girl, I know you've been following the storm that's about to hit us, huh? You planning on going anywhere?" Robertson asked me this while we were on our morning break, but for some reason I wasn't even trying to hear anything about a storm.

Katrina had hit only a few short weeks ago and it seemed unreal that we were sitting up anticipating the wrath of another one, which they chose to name "Rita."

I had been getting glimpses and pieces of the weather reports, but I was trying to avoid the news all together, the death and destruction had me on overload. I just couldn't get into it like some of the others, who eventually began to make me nervous with their concerns.

However, I did go ahead and tune in. I did want to be up on anything serious that they might have to share and I've learned that some news is better getting firsthand, rather than after it's been passed around and spun certain ways.

From the looks of things I needed to stay tuned in a little more than I thought. Rita was growing and moving in without any reservations.

Her exact course was not immediately clarified. Talk of her even grazing Louisiana, being enough to cause almost irreparable damage, had many shuddering at the thought of those poor people being put through such an overwhelming ordeal again.

Ray Nagin, the mayor of New Orleans, had gone on record stating that he would open certain areas that had been hit by Katrina, but with Rita fast approaching, government authorities on all levels asked that he reconsider.

Of course he would and Bridget gave me a call letting me know that they would not be making that trip to New Orleans after all.

She was somewhat disappointed though. When you're in limbo and relying on someone else to provide your needs, it can be hard to accept or get used to when there's a continual 'flip flop' of plans.

Over the next few days worry was more evident with weather reports and it appeared that Galveston, Texas would be Rita's intended target.

Talk of preparing for it and likely damages, depending on the category, became the topic of every discussion. For some reason I still chose to buffer myself from it.

I don't know whether I was trying to will it away or just let it happen when it happened, but I did know that I wasn't going to spend a lot of time sweating it.

Although it was believed that Rita would hit Galveston, Texas, by the weekend, on Monday, September 19, 2005, Galveston's Mayor and city officials were calling for voluntary evacuations of the island.

By Wednesday, September 21, 2005, mandatory orders were issued and the process of moving the sick, disabled and others who would be priority (under the circumstances) were moved out.

This would also be the day that many of the school districts would announce that they'd be closed on Thursday and Friday, in anticipation of families evacuating the storm, which was making meteorologists earn their pay.

There were a couple of different curves and angles that were taking place with Rita. That along with the panic of those in her path made for total hysteria.

Voluntary evacuations were going on with mandatory ones and it soon became a big, grid locked mess.

This was only compounded when Houston's Mayor simultaneously suggested voluntary evacuations and then, mandatory ones, but the highway (I-45) that was being used by both the Galveston and Houston evacuations had traffic bumper to bumper within a few short hours.

This would become a traveler's nightmare. People were sitting in long lines of traffic for hours on end and were barely crawling ten miles.

Gasoline quickly became 'liquid gold.' In such a little time, it was no longer available.

I watched the TV in disbelief as the lines on major highways (I-45, U.S. 290 and SH 249) were packed as far as the eye could see, with frenzied motorists.

U.S. 290 was only a quick jump from me and when traffic from it started blocking my street off, I knew that this would be one heck of an experience.

My sister would call and tell me that my niece and her three children were trying to get out of Beaumont. I told her to have her keep in touch with me and let me know her every move so that I could snatch her up as soon as she made it to Houston.

We played phone tag back and forth and I did finally get to speak with Brenda and told her to catch a bus to Houston and I'd be there to pick her up.

When she called me back it was to deliver the news that all seats were sold out and another bus wouldn't be leaving until about 9:00 a.m. the next morning.

She told me that in the mean time she'd check with friends who might be leaving, to see if they'd have enough room for them.

Calls from concerned friends and loved ones were coming in from everywhere. I could barely hang up the phone before it would ring again.

My younger brother called on one of those occasions and was asking why I hadn't already taken to the road. I explained to him that I had no intentions of getting out in that madness and would just as soon die in the comforts of home, rather than like a dog on the streets. I was too far-gone to be concerned about getting out.

I remained glued to the news reports of people having their cars to stall due to mechanical failure or lack of gasoline and some of the people were passing out and being overcome from the heat.

"Then what are you going to do?" he forcefully stated. "I'm going to stay put. If those people don't hurry and get out of that traffic, they more than likely will be unintended victims of this storm. I'm a lot safer here at home than I'd be on the road right now."

He sighed and said, "So you gone sit there and not try to get out?" I was becoming annoyed now because I know that was what I just heard myself say.

"Yes, under the circumstances it's better and y'all act like people are scared to die or something," I retorted. He grunted and hastily replied, "Sometimes people want you to be around longer and to live life."

"Well, it's not *their* call." After I said this, he abruptly brought our conversation to a close and said that he'd get back with me a little later to see what was going on.

Between watching the news and sleeping, my daughter, Nae-Nae and I remained fairly calm about it all. My oldest, Bianca was a nervous wreck and asked both of us how we could sleep at all knowing that a hurricane was headed our way.

I politely told her that, "My staying awake ain't gone make it go away, so I chose to sleep. Especially since in the times of storms I get some of my best rest."

Nae-Nae assured her that, "I've prayed about it and God knows what he's doing." There was nothing else to be said. We continued to let her pace like a caged animal and lose sleep, but we were not going to be denied.

For the next several hours we would sleep, watch TV and handle the many incoming calls from concerned parties.

It had gotten to the point where I was talking to someone every hour on the hour and they were that much more concerned for us.

I heard from Brenda one more time. She explained that a lady who drives a bus was going to be leaving Beaumont first thing in the morning. I told her to call me as soon as they were on the road so I could be ready to get her and we move on from there, if the roads were safe.

With Houston being the confirmed target for Rita and her category being a five, I was sure to pay close attention to her reach and the possibility of damage.

It was not too good. The map that the weatherman was using showed that if Houston were to take a direct hit the winds in my area could be from 85-100 miles per hour. I live upstairs and recall all too well how they kept urging viewers to remain in the lower section of their homes and to stay away from windows.

I lost out all around. My bedroom has an extremely large and picturesque bay window, with my bed resting in front of it.

The girls have a window that's directly in front of their beds and the living room has an oversized window there too.

Other than the concern that the roof might be torn off and we get exposed to the wind and flying debris, I wasn't in the least bit apprehensive about remaining at home.

Nae-Nae and I both seemed to tire of the news reports and the waiting. She glanced over at me during one of our fed up moments and said, "Mommy, I'm sorry, but I'm just ready for it to hit and be through." All I could do was nod in confirmation.

I double-checked our supplies. I wanted to get a few more gallons of water and batteries. I was contemplating doing that when Bianca quickly entered, saying, "Mommy! Have you seen the traffic in front of the house?"

I thought there might be a wreck or something going on. I rushed outside onto the porch and saw that cars were bumper to bumper. I went down the stairs and walked to the curb and took a glance.

Cars were backed up the entire length of our street. These motorists were attempting to get onto U.S. 290, the highway that was a straight shot for me only hours ago, before news reporters mentioned its easy access.

It seemed that no sooner than available roads were announced, instant gridlock was sprinkled across the lanes. I could hardly believe what I was seeing.

"Darn! That was going to be the route I was going to take to Brenham or College Station. There's no telling how much longer it'll be before it's halfway decent. Girl, do you realize that for this traffic to be backed up all the way to our house, those people are going to be at it for a while?" I said.

"What are you gonna do now?" she asked. I pursed my lips and replied, "I'm going to get some bread and peanut butter and call it a night. I can't stress over things I have no control over."

I went into the house, got my purse and headed out for the store. I had no problem getting out as I was going in the opposite direction of 'fleeing' motorists.

The line seemed to never end. I have lived here for almost nine years and up until today had never seen this much traffic on my street.

It was so bad that even when traffic lights signaled for traffic to move in a certain direction, they couldn't because impatient drivers had blocked intersections completely.

When I saw this, I immediately became angry. I can understand people wanting to get away from an incoming hurricane, especially after what we saw Katrina do, but it made no sense for them to totally disregard all that was right, just because they wanted to be where they were going yesterday.

I told Nae-Nae to hold on because when the light changed, I wasn't going to miss it. She had an "Oh Lord" look on her face and I tapped my fingers on the steering wheel as we waited.

The driver next to me had to have been thinking the same thing as I was because when the light changed he hurriedly entered the intersection and made those seeking to continue the snaking line, wait.

All I had to do was ease into the flow. He had already stopped traffic so all was well with the world. At least until we got to the grocery store.

There were no carts inside and the lines looped up and down the packed aisles. There was no water, no bread, no crackers and the rows and rows of air were something that my mind refused to perceive.

In fact, this store looked as though it had been hit by a hurricane. Being the "closet journalist" that I am, I took my camera with me and began sneaking off shots of the emptied shelves and packed checkout lanes.

In the event that a manager came to me and asked that I not take pictures, I already had my 'independent journalist' line ready for him, but none did so I took a couple and left it alone. I didn't want to push it.

We got the few items that we wanted and I was contemplating buying a bag of wings and doing 'em up real good. The meat manager came over and said, "You always seem to make it in *after* we've had a good sale. What you looking at, those wings?"

I turned and looked at him, saying, "Hey, yeah I was thinking I could get a couple days use out of these. Are they not on sale? Can you reduce the price? With Rita coming and the strong possibility that we'll be without electricity, wouldn't you want to sale them now and not have to worry about throwing them out later?"

He put on a fake disappointed scowl, "Now you know I wish I could, but these were on sale last week, buy one get one free. The only thing I could do is take two dollars off of beef items, but these I don't have control over."

I put on my fake disappointed scowl too and said, "Awww…OK, thank you. Maybe I can catch them on sale the next time."

Nae-Nae rushed past me and practically screamed once she made it to the safety of another aisle. I darted over to her and asked her what was wrong.

"Mommy, you are throwed off! You know you wrong for that little act you put on back there. You gone look all serious, knowin' good and darn well you wanted to tell that man where he could stick those wings."

I couldn't help but laugh with her. When he ran the 'okie doke,' I decided I wasn't going to let it ruffle my feathers any.

Hex, if they wanted to be throwing those wings out in a few days, so be it. We made it in line and the Lunchables that they had on sale, two-for-one were not ringing up at the sale price and rather than have anyone wait for a price check, I told the cashier to take them all off. She acted as if she was mad about it, but I didn't care.

It works my nerves for something to be on sale, but not ring up at the register. We got our goods and headed for the door.

When we got to it, it didn't slide open. "What in the…" I didn't get to finish, one of the employees was at the other door saying, "Miss, we're using this door now," and he beckoned us over there.

I looked upside his head and he finished, "We've reached fire code capacity and we needed to get the numbers down before allowing more to come in."

"Ohhhh…I see. I'm sho' glad nobody was losing it and taking a sister hostage." Maaaan, what I say that for? Nae-Nae skipped to the car and left me by myself.

When I got in the car we couldn't say anything for the first five or ten minutes because we were all over the place, laughing.

She said, "Mommy, when are you gonna stop? You need to quit!" I shook my head and shrugged my shoulders.

"Girl, I don't know, but you know who I belong to so you know I got a double dose. Hex, you've been my daughter all these years, you should know what to expect by now?" I said.

"Naw Shandra, you're full of surprises." By the time we finished our laugh at this little statement, I almost forgot that we were trying to gather items for a hurricane.

We went to another store and every line had at least twenty people waiting in it. It was unbelievable!

I thought about what we needed and looked at the door, I thought about what we needed and looked at the door, I thought about...and by this time Nae-Nae said, "I know good and well you ain't gone wait in these lines for a piece of 'cone-bread'."

She was on a roll today and I wondered whether people thought it inappropriate of us to be laughing and cutting up as we were, under the circumstances.

We didn't seem to care though, because down every aisle we went and with each piece of merchandise we picked up, we said or did something off the wall.

Come to think of it, we might have been burning off some nervous energy. Nothing or no one seemed to be as important as our enjoying this little time together.

The girls talk about me, but "truth be known," they are just like me.

We had all that we needed and were ready to get back to the house. We went through the express lane and it only took about twenty minutes before we made it through the line. That wasn't too bad.

But I was ready to scream and throw a big fit when we were shown yet another door, because they were too full and needed to let some out before allowing more in.

I turned and looked at Nae-Nae and said, "I don't know about you, but this is a sign that it's time for us to head for the Ponderosa. This is the second store that we've been to and had to be ushered out because of over-crowding." "You ain't got to tell me twice," she said, taking the keys from my hand and heading for the car. I was glad that we had gotten in and out and would be in the comforts of home in a few minutes.

The traffic on my street was still horrible I slithered through the back streets until I made it home. I glanced around to be sure that I could go and when I turned to the left I about fell out of the car. A female motorist had gone to the passenger side of her car, pulled down her pants and used it right there in plain view of everyone.

I couldn't believe it and screamed for Nae-Nae to get the camera and take the shot. Hey, she was fair game. Out in the open, in grid locked traffic. OK?

Chapter Nine

With the way that the phone rang off the hook (through the night), it's a wonder that we got any sleep at all. I was still worried about Brenda. I hadn't heard anything else from her and Nita was sure that we would have heard something by now.

It's Friday and in a few more hours we'll be in life or death struggles to defeat Rita or we'll be breathing sighs of relief that she decided to show us mercy.

Mom was worried and I asked Nita not to let her know that with all major highways blocked, I would not be able to get out of Houston.

I told her to think of something else to tell her until I could see what was going to be an absolute. Nae-Nae taped the windows and we ran a check of our survival list again.

I boiled water and filled two plastic containers that could each hold four gallons. I cut up celery stalks to have with my peanut butter and took the last pieces of Popeye's chicken and put them in a plastic bag.

Even the line in there was out the door. We waited about thirty minutes before our order was filled and hot-tailed it back home. The manager stated that they were making on the average about six hundred dollars an hour. I don't find that hard to believe at all.

Bianca was helping friends to secure their belongings, but she checked in with us frequently. We continued to watch each update that the mayor would give and with this last one he advised anyone who had not taken to the road to stay put as this was getting down to the defining hour.

Nae-Nae looked at me a little nervously, but I smiled and continued to keep my 'brave face' on for her. I used the reports of motorists being dehydrated and having to abandon their vehicles on the side of the road as confirmation that we weren't supposed to be out there in it.

Although I didn't want her to know it, I was beginning to worry about whether or not I should try to get her somewhere else.

I was OK and didn't concern myself with *me*, but I did want to be sure that I had done all that I could to have her out of harm's way.

Nissie had called me last night and invited me to go with them up to Tina's, but I didn't want to intrude on their time together.

They would not have seen it like that and she wouldn't have invited me if she didn't mean it, but I didn't want to feel that I was imposing on them.

The initial plan had been for Nae-Nae and Brenda to go to Oklahoma and I stay closer, in the event that relief volunteers were needed.

I was already trained and had put in several clock hours, so it would have been right on time. Nonetheless, I did reconsider evacuating when weathermen kept stressing that Category 4 and 5 hurricanes cause extreme amounts of damage when they hit.

I don't know that I would have been concerned that we were on a bottom floor, then the only worry would have been getting to higher heights once the flooding began.

It was a catch-twenty-two situation. Stay low to the wind and get high from the water.

For some reason I decided to take a peek outside and could see that the sky was changing. It was a little darker in the eastern corner. I could see little particles of flowers and plants being carried away by a mild wind.

The phone rang and I hurried in to answer it. "Hello?" It was Nita. "Shan, we found Brenda. She's in St. Augustine and Annie is going to go and pick her up and take her back to Plano with her. So you can rest about her. Are you able to get out now?"

I was relieved that my niece and her children were safe, but that left Nae-Nae and me to be the center of everyone's worry.

"No, we won't be able to get out there in it. The mayor just came on and asked that anyone who was not already on the highways to stay put. They don't want to take a chance on people being trapped on the roads when she hits. We'll be OK. Please don't let mother worry." I used my 'brave voice' when I said this.

She sighed a little and tried to sound chipper, but I knew that she was a nervous wreck. "OK, Umm...You know you'll have to check in with us hourly, right? If we don't hear from you, then we'll be calling you. If anything happens that you can get out and it's safe, you will take it won't you?"

I laughed to myself and said, "Yeah, but only if it's safe and won't put Nae and me at a greater risk." It was quiet for a minute and then she said, "OK, let me get off of here so I can see if Annie has left to get Brenda yet and we'll check in again in a little bit. I love you girlie."

I fought back tears and said, "I love you too," and then we got off of the phone. I had grown tired of the weather reports so I felt another nap was in order.

A call from Bianca would awaken me from the peaceful sleep that I was in, but I was glad that it gave me the opportunity to tell her to stay put and not leave her whereabouts under *any* circumstance.

She assured me that she wouldn't and we awkwardly ended the call, trying to assure the other that everything would be OK.

The wind had begun to pick up a bit and the sky was a shade or two darker than when I had earlier observed. It was coming, but the 'wait and see' was more than enough to drive someone crazy.

Then came the news of the deaths of twenty-three elderly evacuees, from a nursing home in Bellaire, Texas, they died when the bus that they were traveling in exploded.

It appears that a mechanical problem with the bus sparked a flame and with oxygen in use by some of them, they didn't have a chance. May God forever keep them in peace and keep their families and their loved ones comforted.

Of all the tragedies that had gone on thus far, I believe this is the one that shook me most. It appeared to me that fleeing Rita was causing more damage than possibly riding her out.

We watched as Rita's Category went from a 5 to a 4 and then to a 3. When the meteorologist mentioned that there was a possibility for her to return to a category 4, I was about done and was upset that the mayor was not going to list shelters that he had put in place, publicly.

I can understand that he didn't want people to see it as an alternative to leaving, which he strongly advised, but I did have trouble understanding how those who got caught here in Houston, by no choice of their own, would be forced to ride her out. It seemed insensitive that he could have 'secret shelters,' but given all the lives lost in Katrina and what was being said about Louisiana's mayor, Ray Nagin, I could somewhat see his "better safe than sorry" approach.

Finally at about 4:00 p.m. they started listing the names and addresses of shelters, for those who hadn't gotten out of town and could still make it before nightfall and the ultimate delivery of Rita.

I grabbed a pencil and jotted down the number of the one that was fairly close to me. I ran into the room and told Nae that they had listed a shelter that we could go to. I called and was told that they still had room and that I'd need to bring my own bedding because they were out of cots.

She looked a little unsure at the thought, but quickly received it and I know it was only because she knew that I *needed* her to be OK with it.

I got online and answered email that I had not responded to and began to pack up enough goods to last us the weekend.

I called Nita and told her to tell mother that we were going into a shelter and I would call as soon as I got there.

In my mind I could see her do a cartwheel as she screamed, "Yes! God answered both of my prayers! I got off the phone with Annie not even five minutes ago and she told me that she has Brenda and they're on their way back home. Whew! He delivered both of them. Let me call mother and let her know. That's going to put her at ease. OK, let me let you get out of there. Call me as soon as you make it there and give me all of their information. I love you girl, bye!"

It was about 5:30 p.m. before we had gotten everything together and made it to the shelter. It was at St. Kolbe Catholic Community. When I drove up there people were hanging out on the grounds, smoking, talking and nervously awaiting the storm.

We emptied our belongings at the front desk and waited for them to register us. The Red Cross was responsible for this shelter and that was a plus because I knew that meant they'd have the right connections to whatever it was we needed before, during and after the storm.

I called Nita after we were entered into their system and told her that she'd be able to check on us via their database.

I also gave her their address and phone number to call and check on us, in the event that my much overworked cell phone was charging and I not have the opportunity to call them.

I signed up to be a volunteer while there. I didn't want to sit idle. Anything that I could do to help out would not be a problem for me.

They were assigning ten people to each room. We were in Room 108. The only other occupants were Hispanic. They spoke little to no English and it was rather awkward, but we didn't want them to feel uncomfortable.

We unpacked and kept our things close together. No sooner than we had sat things down and turned to walk out, two of the younger volunteers came in and asked if anyone in the room needed cots.

Nae-Nae and I quickly spoke up. We had blankets and things, but the thought of a cot sounded so much better. Along with the cots, they also brought us bath towels.

OK, it was time to explore the place now. We had the important things taken care of and I needed to know who else was sharing this space with us.

Before I did anything else I called Nita and let her know that we were settled in. She said that mother was elated and we'd continue our contact every hour as planned.

There were already two hundred people here and I wondered how I was going to adjust to going from a Disaster Relief Volunteer to being an evacuee.

It was a rather unsettling feeling, but at the same time I will have lived both sides of the story.

I walked over to one of the many tables and sat down. A lady who introduced herself as Sybil was there. She was from Port Arthur, Texas, one of the areas that would be in the direct line of fire, if Rita decided to head that way.

She told me how they had gotten on the road at 10:00 p.m. on Wednesday and didn't make it to Houston until 7:00 a.m. on Thursday.

She was a little concerned for her daughter and her husband because they wanted to wait before they took to the road and she hoped that they hadn't decided to wait too long.

Our conversation was cut short by shouts of, "You boys cut it out! Break it up!" Our attention was drawn to a crowd of people, one of them being the Red Cross coordinator for the morning, a teen volunteer and two boys who had obviously had a disagreement about something.

One was older and he had his arm wrapped tightly around the younger ones throat. He had such a hold on him that the younger one was a deep red color and I was wondering why no one else was going to the aid of the woman and teen.

I thought about it, but the possibility of being injured in the melee helped me to hold out a little longer and see if it might be handled sooner.

The teen was able to get a good grip on the older one and hold him off until the older woman had pulled the younger boy free and was seeing if he was OK.

He was still gasping for breath and it seemed so strange to watch him go from deep red to light pink again.

The older woman would get on the microphone and ask that the fathers of the two boys who were fighting come see her.

As it turned out, both boys were there with their divorced or otherwise single mother. I sat in amazement at first and then I was somewhat relieved. When Sybil turned to me and whispered, "See, it ain't just *us*." I knew why the fact that these were two little white boys gave me a little peace.

With the way that the media had been portraying Katrina evacuees and making them appear to be ruthless hoodlums, there was no shame in my not wanting this act of violence to be chalked up to <u>US</u>.

I was stewing over the photographs that had been circulating on the Internet. One was of a young black man wading through chest deep water, carrying goods in his hand and in a garbage bag. His caption described him as "looting."

The other was of a couple, who appear to be white, wading through chest deep water and carrying goods, just as this young man was doing, but in their caption it read that they were "finding" food.

Help me understand, OK? How in the hex was he "looting," but they were "finding"? Either they're ALL looting or they're ALL finding, Right?

After rapper Kanye West made his 'statement heard around the world,' that, "President Bush don't care about black people," and made reference to those infamous photographs, the media outlets that were responsible issued statements.

The API pulled the photograph and apologized for what seemed to be inferred by the photograph. However, the AP photographer stated that his photograph was accurate, as he *saw* the young man break into the deserted store and take the items.

I'd almost believe that, untouched. However, my problem with it is this, sensationalism sales and it would have been more powerful for him to have gotten the shots of this brother throwing a brick through the window and then entering the store or kicking the door in and taking what he wanted.

That would have spoken loud and clear, without a caption, but he gets one 'lone' shot of the man *after* he has left the *burglarized* store and wants it to stand alone in his insistence that the man was 'looting'? Riiight.

About an hour after we were comfortable and getting beyond the fracas that had broken out, a lady and her family came in. I lost all train of thought when I saw that she had written their names and social security numbers on their arms.

I had made reference to doing it, but actually seeing it on someone and realizing that it might be necessary for official identification of their bodies to take place, I was no good for a few minutes.

A chill went up my spine and the thought of dying became more real than it had ever been before.

I was sure to make note of a very aggressive Hispanic lady who was there. Mary Jones, a double-evacuee, told me that she had gotten ugly with her over the TV channels that were being watched.

Mary is a 'seasoned' soul with a very gentle and inviting spirit. I couldn't even fathom anyone speaking out of place to her, but she didn't have anything to worry about. I was here now and whoever felt the need to disrespect her would have to deal with me as well.

Her son Karl was with her too, but some things women can convey a little better than men. He cherished his mother and you could tell it through their interactions and manner of speaking and staying close to one another.

He had been relocated to Arkansas, when news of Rita heading for Texas became clear. He had been given an apartment and was looking to start work.

Once he heard that his mother would have to evacuate again, he stopped, dropped and ran to be with her. She had already told him that she would travel to him and to not jeopardize keeping the apartment or work, but he would not hear of his mother traveling alone.

They were on their way to College Station when they were told about the shelter. They were quite happy with that. They were tired, hungry and frustrated beyond belief.

I carefully eyeballed the woman who had over-stepped her bounds with her. I was sizing her up and making note of who was with her.

She was a tough-looking, male feature having chick. She walked and carried herself like everybody owed her something.

I looked over at Nae-Nae and said, "If she even looks at me wrong, Rita will have arrived here in Houston." Nae-Nae was checking her out herself because she knew I didn't play about 'ol folks' and children.

We had talked and visited with a few of the evacuees, but by far Mary and Karl were two of the ones we enjoyed the most.

After they called it a night I decided that I was going to try and "catch forty." It was late and I didn't want to disturb the other occupants of the room.

Too late! When we got to the room it was pitch black! She nudged me and said, "Ooooo…" and a tiny little voice yelled out, "Hi-looow!"

We were too through after that. Nearly everyone in the room burst out laughing at that darling little voice and whoever it was who owned it.

To think that would be the *only* disturbance we'd cause was asking too much. Nae-Nae's cot was like taking and rubbing pieces of sandpaper against each other.

The scratchy, squeaky sound was magnified in this absolutely quiet room. I was laughing into my hands to keep from waking anyone else up.

She had no control over the loud cot, but I could control my laughing, somewhat. No sooner than I had contained my laughter, she rolled over and said, "Mommy, you won't believe this, but I gotta use it." I dared not respond to her. If I had, we would have gotten put out of the shelter this night because I was practically wheezing by now.

She went and came back. After a few minutes she was settled down and asleep. I lay there thanking God that we were safe, that my niece and her children were out of harm's way and I prayed that if and when I awoke in the morning, the devastation wouldn't be as bad as Katrina. Then I cried.

Around 3:00 a.m. I heard the window shaking and vibrating. I was sure that it was only Rita making her call. I was near it, but since I wasn't directly in front of it, I didn't bother repositioning myself.

I lay there for a while longer and then got up because I couldn't get back to sleep. When I rounded the corner to the

TV area, I saw that several of the residents had stayed up to monitor news reports.

When I heard them mention Beaumont, Texas, I moved a little closer and learned that a hotel had their windows to be blown out and that Houston had been spared Rita's wrath.

It was Port Arthur and Beaumont that would be torn apart and mishandled by her unpredicted last minute swerve to the right.

Although my niece and her children made it out, her mother and sister had stayed behind and she didn't know whether or not they had gotten out in time.

I called Nita to let her know that Beaumont took it on the chin and cautioned her that maybe someone should let my niece know, so that she wouldn't become too stressed out if she saw it on the news and wondered where her mother and sister might be. She agreed and I went ahead and got off with her. I wanted to try and get some of the sleep that I had missed out on over the past forty-eight hours.

A big pop would shake me from my sleep, but it wasn't enough to make me abandon it all together. I rolled over and checked on Nae-Nae. She was still asleep, with the covers pulled over her head.

I finally arose at about 5:30 a.m. It was a little darker than I remembered and I soon discovered that the power had gone out.

That loud noise that I heard was the generator blowing out. No lights meant no air and no charger for my cell phone. It also meant no clear breathing for me if it got too stuffy.

I've been asthmatic long enough to know that cool air and easy breathing go hand in hand. I called Nita to let her know that we were without power and that not hearing from me would only mean that my cell phone was unable to be charged.

I also reminded her to use the number of the shelter in the event that a message to me was a must. We were 'official' evacuees, so we were in their database if they needed to contact us.

At about 6:30 a.m. the lights were back on and I made a beeline to the shower. I about passed out when I found out that there were only two of them and that there was NO privacy between them and the restroom.

I didn't care though. I wanted to have some warm water roll down my back to invigorate my tired, aching, joints and bones.

If some of my coworkers were here, they'd be sick with laughing at me. I washed down the shower nozzle and sprayed down the walls and everything before I showered. All Nae-Nae could say when I told her was, "Ma, you need some help, for real."

I won't lie though, regardless of the circumstances, it felt good to be in fresh, clean clothes. I went out and a comforting breeze followed by droplets of rain soothed me.

I took a few shots with my digital camera and captured some very nice pictures of the scenery around us and the mood of the sky. I pulled out my notebook and pen to continue recording my journey.

I met a gentleman named Jose Castro, his wife, their three sons, son-in-law, daughters-in-law and the parents of the in-laws.

There were many of them who traveled together from Santa Fe, Texas. They had gotten word that their home was OK and the wind only toppled over insignificant things.

He told me about another lady that he met from Port Arthur, who went to an all black school that he used to frequent for their sports activities.

He glowed when he told me that they talked for about two hours and how it helps when you run across 'good' people, even under these circumstances.

He had me laughing most of the time that we talked. He kept cracking jokes about how lucky his wife was to have married him. Of course she'd look at him crazy and roll her eyes.

We ran into a stalemate when he found out that I'm originally from Oklahoma. He was sitting there big as day in a Longhorns T-shirt. Oops!

He joked that we'd have to part friendship and be done with it. He also said he was glad that I gave him something to think about from now on, when the OU Sooners and Texas Longhorns would meet.

"Friend, when you write about this damn Mexican, be sure you spell it right. It's not M-e-x-a-c-a-n. It's M-e-x-i-c-a-n." After he said this I dropped my pen onto the notebook and howled.

He had cut up from the time I sat down next to him until they headed back home. On the occasions when he'd say something outlandish to me, he'd lean in closer and say, "Crazy Mexican."

By the time all was said and done, he was a "Crazy Mexican," "Damn Mexican," "Bad Mexican," "Mean Mexican," and "Lazy Mexican."

His family just looked at him and shook their heads. Some shared that I was in trouble the minute that I sat down and let him start talking.

They were very close-knit and loving people. You could tell in the way that they paid so much attention to one another and tuned everyone else out when one or the other was sharing.

They had nice, home cooked meals that they all sat down and enjoyed together. It really warmed my heart to see them conveying that family bond.

The hour finally came for them to get back on the road and he walked around to all of those whom he had spoken to (over the course of time that he was here) and shook their hand.

He was sure to tell everyone who would listen that it was he who taught me how to spell 'Mexican' correctly. He came over, looked me in the eye and said, "You're good people. I knew that when I saw your smile and had your soul said anything different to me, I would have never talked to you. It was a pleasure talking to you and knowing that when we beat Oklahoma, you'll have to think about me." He hugged me and I wished them a safe trip back home.

He saw that I was a little misty eyed and said, "Awww, don't you start any of that," and went to join his family in the car. We'll meet again "Tilo," count on it.

Soon after he left, Mary's daughter called. She was quite glad to hear from her. When she got off with her she sighed, "I've talked to everyone, who I *needed* to," turned her phone off and went to take some medicine.

I sat and talked with her son and some of the others who had come over and joined us. There was a lady there with a son named "J-maine". Theresa and her 'baby doll,' daughter, Diamondneeshay. She also had two older sons with her. They seemed shy and kept to themselves most of the time. It so happens that "J-maine's" mother and Theresa are cousins.

After a while, I went and called Bridget to see how they were doing and found that she was visiting her mother and sister in Laredo, Texas. When she learned that I was in a shelter, she spoke of the irony of going from volunteer to evacuee.

"God bless you Shan. You were so good to us and we'll never be able to forget you and all that you've done for us. I was thinking about you yesterday and it seems that when I think about you a lot, you call. I was telling my mother how sweet you were to us and had gone and gotten us so many things that we needed. I hadn't seen them since Katrina, so you know it was long overdue," she said.

It was strange that we were all calling their names (Katrina and Rita) like they were 'good' friends of ours. As long as I live, I don't believe I'll ever forget the names of two of the most crippling storms to have come this way in a long time.

"We were interviewed and will be in the New York Times. A photographer is supposed to be on the way, now," she excitedly told me.

"Hey now! You'll be the second set of evacuees that I personally know to have done it. Mary and Karl Jones, a mother and son who are here, interviewed with USA Today."

"Shandra, it was so nice. We got to tell them of how we were business owners and although we didn't have millions of dollars in insurance coverage, we were hoping to be OK and get back to a place and time when we were on our feet and doing for ourselves, without relying on the aid of government. They need to know that not all of us are as the media is portraying us."

I let her finish and added, "You're absolutely right and someone, somewhere is going to read that article and offers will begin to pour in to you all. Wait and see."

"Thank you Shandra. You are so optimistic and keep telling us to hang in there when we feel tired and frustrated with all that is going on around us. You know what? It's not like we want to act like there's no one else who needs help. We're blessed and we know it. I was sure to tell Keith that when we passed a homeless man on the street today."

We chatted a little while longer and ended with her taking me up on my offer of having their stories told and in their own words.

My next endeavor would be going home to see whether we had power and whether or not a strong wind came along and did anything extra to it.

We passed blown over signs, split utility poles and knocked down trees and we weren't quite sure what we might find once we reached home.

Everything was fine, but the lights weren't on. We didn't have a reason to stay, so we headed back to the shelter.

On the way back I noticed a few motorists in line at a gas station. I was almost to a half tank and knew that being able to fill it up would be absolutely wonderful.

I quickly turned the corner and took my place in line. It moved rather fast, but I had to pull in on the opposite side of my gas tank. When I made it to the pump I tried to pull close enough to pull the hose over to that side, but it wasn't long enough.

I went to the lady behind me and let her know that I was going to be backing up and pulling in the correct way.

In the meantime another pump in front of us became free so she went to that one and I turned around. A gentleman thought that I had cut the line from the other side and yelled. "What the fuck!" He was acting rather childishly, as if he wasn't going to let me pull up and get my gas.

At this point I had my fill of the ignorance and mass hysteria that some of these people were creating and I jumped out of the car, rushing over to his side yelling, "What in the hell are you beefing for? I've been here! I only turned around because my gas tank is on the other side! I'm getting my freaking gas and then you can pump yours!" Nae-Nae almost laid down right there in the parking lot when he started rolling up his window real fast, as if anticipating a blow from me.

She pulled herself together and ran over to me and asked me to get back into the car.

As if that weren't enough, I saw the lady who had been behind me talking to some guys who were questioning whether I had jumped the line and I politely went over to put an end to this nonsense.

I looked at each of them and said, "Let's get this straight here and now. I jumped in line nowhere. I was *already* in line, in front of her. I pulled in on the wrong side of my gas tank and turned around. That was all that I did. The two of us were the next ones in line and we got to use the pumps. Only difference is that she pulled up to this next one that became available and let me turn around like I needed to."

They shook their heads like they understood and I hopped back into my car, ready to get away from here.

It had gotten wild. People were outside of their cars and were re-directing people who they thought had jumped the line and two or three different arguments broke out.

People were acting like they didn't want to move and let customers who had already received their services out. If I got started, there would be no turning back so I sat looking daggers at those who were blocking me until they started swinging a few turns and allowed me to exit.

We were about five or ten minutes down the street when we heard sirens blaring and police officers racing to that location. Whew! This would be another time that I was glad that we were quick on our feet and out of the area.

There had been reports all day long of the violence at the pumps and arrests that had been made, but I would have never thought that we'd have to worry about it.

I was surprised that this station even had any gas, all of the other stations and stores were completely out. Maybe it was assumed that they had none and only when people saw others fueling up, did they realize that they had a few drops left.

We went to another store to get a few things that we might need before tomorrow and I was still on a mission to find Karl the kind of cigarettes that he smokes.

Two stores did not carry them or didn't have them and I did not want to go back with no cigarettes for him. It was better for his lungs, but he was nervous, anxious and so unsure of how things would be, that he really needed his puff time.

Finally, at the last store that I stopped at, they carried his brand. He gave me enough to get him as many packs as he could get.

I kindly had Nae-Nae to get what she had come in for and we were too glad to be on our way back to the shelter.

When we got there and saw police officers and an ambulance, we were fearful. As it turns out, someone who didn't have his meds had an anxiety episode.

"What a time and place to have one," I said, while looking over at Nae-Nae, making sure she was OK.

Chapter Ten

Once situated inside again, we relayed the events that took place while we were gone. Most of those who were listening found it incredible that people were losing their heads like that.

Many of the families began to check out and return to the road. Houston dodged a bullet and they wanted to be able to get back to lives that were only mildly interrupted.

Many school districts had already announced closings until the middle of the following week. That was good for all involved, except for when the time comes to make those days up (insert sarcasm).

It was after dinner, at about 6:30 p.m., when the first of three more buses rolled in. We had no idea that they were coming and were thinking that it would be nice and slow with so few remaining.

After that, two more pulled in and we knew it was crunch time. They made it in just in time to receive hot dogs and beans.

Had they been an hour or so earlier, they would have been able to enjoy some pit grilled pork chops. I don't eat beef or pork, and those who know me know that I wouldn't have eaten these unless I knew the one who prepared them (personally) and was able to see how many times he washed his hands. No offense meant. That's just me.

Red Cross workers slowly but surely got them entered into their records and assigned them rooms. With this many new faces around, we knew that we'd probably be with people who might not be on the same schedule as we were. I basically told Nae-Nae that I was going to sit up all night, but would watch over her as she slept.

Quite a few of the new arrivals were content with getting a bite to eat and retreating to their designated rooms.

Some remained outside to smoke and enjoy the gentle weather, while others stayed watching the news, wanting to know when they could return home.

Texans were going to be able to return home according to where they lived and how much their area was damaged.

Sunday was the day scheduled for me and that was fine because we were without power anyway. Others didn't care what was being asked, they left anyway.

I'm sure most were concerned about getting home and looking into their homes and making sure that everything was OK.

I glanced up and saw Nae-Nae looking at me in an odd kind of way. After a man using a walker passed us, she said, "He was getting up and looked over here at me and asked me if you were my mother and I told him you were."

I shot a look in the direction that she had leaned her head and saw a short, husky kinda guy going to get a drink.

I laughed and said, "Claude have mercy! He was the one who asked if I was your mom?" she said nothing and nodded her head.

"If he don't get somewhere and sit down. How you gone be up in a shelter getting' ya' mack on?" Her eyes got real big and I knew that was our sign that something was up.

I stopped talking immediately and he walked up behind me and said, "I ain't gone even lie. I don't need this." I thought he was talking about the services of the shelter.

We both looked at him quizzically. Then he touched the walker that he was using. "This, I don't need *this*."

I threw my hand up and said, "No need to confess today. That's between you and your maker."

He leaned in and said, "Shhh…Naw let me explain." I turned my head and was pretending that I was tuning him out. Nae-Nae was over there about to burst. She kept listening.

"See I found this leaning against the wall at the George R. Brown Convention Center. I figured I could stay in those long behind lines or use it to get moved to the head of the line."

When he said this I shrieked so loud that everyone in the center turned and looked at us. Nae-Nae was gasping for air and fanning herself.

One of the men who came in with him said, "Boy what are you saying to them? Hex, she over there screaming like that, it better be good."

I started waving him away and said, "G'wont on! I'm through with you. Move around now please." He grabbed my hand and through grunted laughs said, "Awww…Naw pretty lady, don't do me like that. Please let me stay here with y'all." I looked over at him and replied, "You know yo' butt needs help, right?"

He looked around real sly-like and said, "*That's* what I'm trying to get. Now I was being honest. I coulda kept lying and playing hurt, but I told the truth."

I leaned in closer to him and said, "Do me a favor, don't make any more confessions to me. How about that?" I was sure that someone might come over and ask us to find somewhere else to be because we roared like crazy after I said that.

That basically was the deal closer for the evening because it was getting late and people had started to retire. Nae-Nae and I just sat there chatting.

A man came over and asked if a seat near us was taken. I told him it wasn't and he looked as if he had just had a shower.

He was putting lotion on his arms and feet. I had kicked my shoes off and had them resting in a chair. He glanced over at them and said, "If one of these mugs in here gets hungry, you better hide ya' feet."

Nae-Nae shot daggers at him and was about to say something when I interrupted her and asked him, "Excuse me?" and slid them back in my shoes.

He smiled and said, "I was complimenting you on how pretty your feet are. I was saying if one of these men got hungry you'd need to hide 'em because they sho' look good enough to eat."

Embarrassed I said, "Ohhh...OK. I thought you were being funny and don't be looking at my feet. I don't think I bothered to lotion them after I got out of the shower earlier."

He grinned and said, "When they as pretty as that, they don't have to have lotion. Put it back up here and let me see. They look soft as a baby's bottom."

I put one of them up there for him to feel. He rolled his eyes to the back of his head and smacked his lips, saying, "Umm...umm...ummm! They're bunion free and smooth on the bottom too. Hot dayum!"

Nae-Nae leaned over and said, "OK, you can put it down now." He looked at her surprised and asked, "I can't lotion your mama's feet?"

She snapped her baby hazels on him and said, "That's up to her, but you don't need to do all of that pawing in the meantime."

I looked over at her and winked. "That's right baby, show him how we roll up in here." He smiled when I said that and chuckled, "Ain't nuthin' wrong with that. She's supposed to look out for her mama."

I cleared my throat and said, "But umm...you can gone ahead and lotion my feet. I'll give you that honor." I couldn't say it fast enough. He picked up the lotion and took the top off before I had the chance to change my mind.

He put a good amount in his hands and tore into my overworked foot like crazy. Nae-Nae was checking out the expression on my face and knew that mom was in the zone right about now.

This rascal was working the hex outta my foot. He has had some practice with this and I don't care, who, what, when, where, how, or why, but I was glad that he had gotten the experience.

He would slide up my whole foot on one side and go back down on the other side. He took his thumbs and went from the heel of my foot to the top of my toes. He bent my toes back and forth, side to side and wiggled them as if to shake stress or fatigue from them.

I got quiet as a church mouse. Nae-Nae started laughing and said, "Ma, you are no more good are you?" I didn't even look over there at her, but said, "You already know."

He continued to crack jokes about things that had happened to him in his life and formally introduced himself as Donald.

He was very entertaining and the three of us sat there for about another thirty minutes as he took each of my feet and worked it like he was getting paid for it.

The night shift supervisor finally told us that it was time for 'lights out' and we retreated to our respective pods.

Nae-Nae and I didn't want to stay in ours and decided we'd sleep in one where a lady had a very big room and a TV. We went in and played cards, but the sleepy monster was soon calling our names.

I had already told her that at the crack of day we would be saying our "Good-byes" and heading for the hills.

It was hard for me to sleep because it felt like the church was hanging meat in it overnight. No amount of cover kept me warm enough.

I got up a time or two and walked around, but none of it was enough to help me go back in and get to sleep immediately.

As a new day peeked out over the horizon, I found myself overcome with extra heavy eyelids and crawled back on the mattress next to Nae-Nae and went to sleep.

The birds chirping outside the windows and the sunlight sneaking in helped me to spring into action and get ready to leave here once Nae-Nae awoke.

I had gathered my things and placed them neatly to the side. I went into the restroom and got fresh and clean for a new day and waited for my 'new' friends to start appearing, so that we could let them know that we were leaving.

Remembering that I had said that we'd be making our exit as soon as day broke, Nae-Nae appeared at the end of the room, looking for me.

I stood up and walked over to her. "You ready?" I asked. "Already," was her response. We went to the room where the rest of our things were and waited outside the door while debating whether or not we wanted to awaken anyone who might still be sleep.

"Girl, we are getting ready to leave. There's no other way around it. Let's just go in, grab our things as quietly as possible and clear out."

She said nothing and nodded her approval, while at the same time motioning for me to open the door. We looked at one another and in our minds counted to three. I swung the door open and we eased our way over to our side of the room.

We went through there with a swiftness. We had everything bagged and 'readst' to go in no time. The other occupants of the room barely stirred. We were glad for that.

We walked out to the car and loaded it up. The curious looks and "Y'all leaving?" greeted us as we left and as we came back in.

Either of us would smile and say, "Yes, we're going home." I can't find words to describe what hearing that did to my soul.

"We're going *home*." How blessed we were that we still had one to go to. It was only an upstairs, two bedroom, one bath, four windows having, small place, but it's home and it has been for the past nine years.

I'm in one of the better school districts in Houston, live in a very decent part of town and know many of my neighbors by sight, if not by name.

We've had our share of anxious moments when a car was broken into, neighbors were disagreeing or one or two "unknowns" happened upon the property, but for the most part I don't believe any of that compares to the wonders of what Rita could have done to us.

We didn't have long to wait before Miss Mary surfaced. She came down the stairs smiling, as was common place with her, and said, "Are y'all getting ready to leave now?"

I struggled through tears and said, "Yes ma'am. We're getting ready to go and let Rita be behind us now. You still have my number, right?"

She looked over at Nae-Nae and said, "Yes I do. I'm going to miss y'all so much. Y'all are some very kindhearted people and I know I won't be able to forget you." She hugged Nae-Nae and then me.

"Miss Mary, let me get your number now so I can have it in my phone book. What is it?" As she called it out I dialed it and left this message, "Miss Mary, this is Shandra. I'm standing right here next to you, making sure that you know that I have your number. We enjoyed you and Godspeed with everything that you do. We'll miss you and Karl. Please keep in touch."

After I ended the message I hung it up and hugged her again. I moved faster now because it was hard to tell these people "bye" when for one fateful weekend we were all a family and looking out for one another like we were destined to.

Theresa and her cousin caught me on the way out, to be sure that I'd remember to check with the phone and light companies about connecting service to their new apartments.

They had been under the impression that I was passing through too, but when they learned that I was a resident, they were somewhat relieved that they could count on me to help them in any way that I could.

I'd have the next two days off from work and I was hopeful that it would require an overdose of sleep and relaxation.

It only felt right after all that I had found myself doing, seeing and hearing over the past few weeks. Heaven knows that laundry was long overdue and I could probably stand to spruce my room up a little bit.

It got to the point where I felt selfish when I'd think of the small things that I needed to do, to get back on track, when so many would have to abandon all that they had come to know and without being able to prepare for it first.

I actually made it home and did nothing but jump straight in the shower, scrub head to toe, then toe to head and changed out the linen on my bed and went for what I knew.

I cried myself to sleep because I knew what was ahead of me and I knew the constant reminders of Katrina and Rita would forever be a pain in my heart.

The TV was on, but I didn't care to watch it and did everything that I could to drown out the comparisons that news anchors were making between the two storms.

Katrina left a devastating death toll and mass of destruction, whereas Rita was a little kinder and gentler. I wanted to hear no more of the dead bodies that were being found in homes, attics, rooftops, on city streets – in plain view of passersby or the cost it would take to make New Orleans "great" again. Somehow the "Big Easy" turned out to be anything but that.

The talk of corruption, killings, sex, drugs and other illicit goings on, had some evacuees certain that God was exacting His vengeance on a lawless, morally bankrupt and wicked city.

Sodom and Gomorrah quickly come to mind when one has the occasion to think of how He destroyed cities in order for His power and words to be feared and kept sacred.

It is not my intent to condemn or pass judgment on anyone (person or thing). However, I am a firm believer in what is corrupt and unjust meeting a timely and well-deserved end.

I say "well deserved" only because if the hand of God has caused anything NOT to be, it had to have been because it was earned.

The love for New Orleans and its occupants should not be cast aside and the hopes and beliefs that the message in the storm(s) have been received and duly noted might be one of the best assets of rebuilding.

A teacher at school happened to share with me that a friend had told her that the storms had come to 'punish' the evildoers who had their hands in on slavery and the mistreatment of blacks and was forcing a "reconstruction" period as was done many years ago.

I'm not going to knock anyone's personal beliefs as to why this all happened. I won't try to cram mine down their throat either, but I do hope that others begin to heed the signs of the times and how life as we know it seems to be on a collision course with damnation.

So many catastrophes, man made and by natural occurrence, yet every day that we live and breathe has been taken for granted.

Only through these occurrences do we suddenly find the nerve to seek help or to be a blessing to someone. If WE could learn to be considerate, kind, tolerant and supportive of one another *EVERY* day, this place that we call home might not be so bad off.

When Katrina Stood Down We Came Running, But Rita Tripped Us

By no stretch of the imagination do I want to imply that I have *all* of the answers to the world's problems, but I have a grand belief that communication is the key to bridging gaps and bringing about change.

This world isn't just yours or mine, It's **OURS** and in order to exist and co-exist peacefully and happily, it will take common ground, sacrifice and a fight to the finish, but not to see who finishes first.

What I have seen and been a part of has touched me beyond the realms of simple understanding. I've shared what I had and now I want to share with you what others, evacuees of Katrina, Rita, or both, have lived.

Know that because of this, I'll never be the same and thankfully, I don't want to be.

Theresa Ward is a fast talking, wide-eyed, petite woman, who possesses a very sociable and inviting spirit. When I first saw her at the shelter, during Rita's reign, she was in the company of her miniature-doll of a daughter, Diamondneeshay.

She had her purse on her arm and a small bag of goodies in the other. Circus Peanuts and Ramen Noodles were among them.

She spoke of how the noodles could be eaten every single day, as long as she had her hot sauce to go with them. Twizzlers were her second most favorite food and she'd consume plenty of those as well.

She was rather lively and expressive when she spoke, but when it came to remembering how she was doing before and after the hurricanes, she would slow down a bit and become somewhat reflective and subdued.

Obvious signs that she had yet to come to terms with all that had come about and where she presently found herself and her children.

Any other time you might not be able to associate sadness or defeat with her. However, this time it's all too evident and I look at this smooth skinned, dark chocolate woman, with a beautiful smile, snappy attitude and wonder whether she'll ever be able to put this all behind her and press forward.

She'd have a thousand-watt glow when speaking of how she had just finished creating many adorable barrettes and hair bows, for little girls. She was hoping to build a business on that when Katrina happened.

She went into intricate detail of the colors, designs and time that was spent on each one, almost as if she was verbally walking me through her creating it.

I leaned over and said, "Theresa, you'll be able to start over and the need for pretty hair bows and barrettes didn't disappear when your creations did. Mothers are still going to want to have their babies dolled up and looking pretty. Once you get settled and have the extra money again, don't let your dream die. There are flea markets and boutiques that would gladly carry them. Just stop focusing on the other right now and concentrate on where you want to be a year from now. OK?"

She nodded her head and said, "I'm going to do better. It's just like nobody knows or understands what it's been like for us, but I know that God is going to see me through this, just like He has everything else that I've ever gone through in my life."

I smiled at her and said, "Now *that's* what I'm talking about. I never thought I'd ever be in a shelter either and here I am."

I told her that the Waiver that I prepared for Katrina and Rita evacuees, who I was going to be introducing via the book, was finished and as soon as she was ready, I'd be dropping it off to her. She was ready to roll.

Theresa's Story

Shandra: Did you evacuate immediately?

Theresa: Yes, I was too scared not to.

Shandra: What went through your mind when you did?

Theresa: Fear of death. Not knowing if I would ever be able to see my children, friends or other loved ones. Just death itself and being hurt or losing one of my children.

Shandra: How many are in your family?

Theresa: Six (6)

Shandra: Did all of you make it out?

Theresa: Yes and No. My oldest son (age 21) stayed behind. That was very frightening for me and I was so worried about where he was and whether or not he was in a safe area.

Shandra: Have you heard from other family members who didn't travel with you?

Theresa: It took about two weeks before I heard from my son. If you could only imagine the pain that was placed in my heart, or the fear in my mind during that time. The trauma was truly an experience that no individual would ever want to endure.

Shandra: Theresa, What was life like for you before Katrina?

Theresa: It was pleasant. I was employed and my family and dear friends surrounded me. My children were doing better in school and transportation was readily available. Life was "free."

Shandra: What is it like as a result of Katrina?

Theresa: I am jobless. I have limited family members and although I am living in an apartment, as the old saying goes "There's no place like home." I am accustomed to public transportation, but in the area that I'm currently in, it's scarce. My children have anticipated our getting back to New Orleans.

Shandra: So you're currently in an apartment and not a local shelter?

Theresa: Yes, I have an apartment on the Northwest side of Houston.

Shandra: If they were to rebuild New Orleans successfully, would you go back? Why or why not?

Theresa: Yes! Yes! Yes! If I could, I'd fly on an airplane, on that day. I'd surely be back home if the opportunity presented itself. I miss home. There's no place like home. There's no place like home. There's no place like home.

Shandra: What is it you'd tell people about Hurricane Katrina and the way that things were handled by local, state and federal entities? Could it have been better?

Theresa: The only thing that I can say is, if you are told to evacuate from a hurricane, please follow instructions immediately! Your life depends on it. Once the mayor (Ray Nagin) announced that the residents of New Orleans needed to evacuate, I felt they should have. He could have taken action earlier than he did.

Shandra: What is it that you'd like to share about this experience and where you are right now, emotionally, spiritually, etc?

Theresa: I feel as though I am walking without direction.

Shandra: Any other closing comments you'd like to make?

Theresa: Yes, I need to get home real soon.

Today, October 22, 2005, almost two months to the day that Hurricane Katrina roared through Louisiana, I made it a point to speak with Bridget again.

When we last spoke she was in New Orleans. They were checking on the damage to their home. They live on the West Bank and by the grace of God, were spared the more severe forms of damage and destruction.

Their house sustained a few missing shingles from the roof, some water damage and mold, but it was livable and would take less time to get back to the way they wanted it to be, rather than sit in a city and state that didn't hold their hearts and mind.

A smile came over my face as her familiar accent answered to my buzz. "Hello," she said. "Bridget?" She paused for a second, as if trying to catch on to my voice. "Is this Vanessa?" she asked.

I laughed and joked, "You mean you've forgotten me already? This is Shandra." We both chuckled and she responded, "Ohhhh hi! I'm so glad that you've called me and I'm still in New Orleans. How are you doing?"

"I'm doing fine, thanks. So how are you guys doing? You know it's been a little longer than we normally go without speaking and I wanted to check in on ya' to be sure that all was OK."

"Yes, yes, yes…It has been long, but so much is going on and my relatives are calling my house 'command central.' We received little damage and those of them who needed to store their belongings, have been storing them here and they all come here when they make trips in to move it into storage or whatever."

I then asked, "So does that mean that you guys will remain there in Louisiana?" Without a second wind, she stated, "Yes, we will be here. You know my older daughters have decided to stay there in Houston. We made sure that they were situated in their own place and had reliable transportation before we came back and started doing this all over again. Shandra, I thank God for how he has spared us. Out of all of my relatives, we were the only ones who had a home to come back to and live in."

"Bridget, I'm so glad for you and I pray that He continues to keep you all where you need to be. Not everyone wanted to leave New Orleans forever and some were able to suffer this loss and know that it didn't hold anything else for them." I commented.

"I know. The girls didn't seem interested in being here and I'm so bent out of shape about it. I really wanted them to be here too. I don't know if they are glad to be in their own place and away from me or if I'm making too much out of it because I wanted them to be here with me." We both let out a hearty laugh.

"Bridget, I believe younger people handle things somewhat differently than we do. It could be that they aren't ready to see what they've been able to see on the news for the past two months. It's still very new and real to them and they need to distance themselves from it. Once they've been away from 'home' a while longer and are able to miss your 'motherly' ways, they may very well want to be back there once reconstruction and a better cosmetic view is evident. You think?"

She sighed and said, "I know that's probably true, but you know how it is when you worry about your babies. Even my mother told me that I would never know what it was like for them. They live in a different part of Louisiana and they didn't get out when my husband and I did. I know that there will be some things that will never come to reality for me like it did for them, but this experience will leave none of us the same."

"You're absolutely right and I believe that it was meant for us to meet. We had just completed training and I was adamant that we come down to the area to see if we could come across evacuees and offer up our help or to touch base with their suffering and let them know that we were here and willing to help out. I'm so glad that we did because it has done wonders for my heart to still be able to talk to you all and to know that you're really OK." I can't even describe the feeling that came over me after I said this, but my eyes did tear a bit.

"Shandra, I don't ever intend to lose contact with you. I don't care how long it is before we can get on the phone and speak to one another, I still want to have that there and utilize it as much as possible," she happily offered up.

I smiled and said, "Well, with both of us doing it there really won't be a time when we don't know how the other is coming along. While I have you on, let me let you know what I'm doing and you tell me whether or not you want to do it. Remember when I was telling you that I was going to write a book about 'Katrina'?"

"Ummm...hmmm," she said. "Well, I've already started it and have made much progress. I've sent out the packets that I want participants to answer and I was seeking an address for you so that I could get one in the mail to you as soon as possible. Are you still interested in having your story told?"

"Yes, absolutely! I'd love to do that for you. I believe it would be good for everyone to be able to see how some things went down. Do you have a fax machine? I was going to say that I could give you my fax number and have you send them, but if you don't let me give you my post office box number and the address to my house. When I get them, I will set aside the time to dedicate my full attention to them and get them right back to you."

After she finished that statement I reached for a pen and readied myself to take the addresses. I was on a red light and hoped that it wouldn't change until I was done.

"OK Bridget, I got that and it's a basic questionnaire, but please add as much as you'd like. I don't mind. This is *your* story, *your* way and I want to represent you to the fullest with what I present to a reading audience. The media can't portray this any better than you can and *that's* what I want. Please send a picture that you'd like for me to add to your section. I want to be able to put faces to the stories that I'm sharing. I want you to never be forgotten because your story or picture has been etched into the hearts and minds of those who'll be made privy to it. You know what? I'm going to send a couple extra for you to pass on to other friends or family who might want to share their story. Once I get those back I can add them and be ready for the next ones. OK?"

"OK, I'll look for it. In December, we will be celebrating Christmas at our house. I will be sure to get a picture of all of us then and have you put it in the book too."

I found it absolutely amazing that in spite of all of the misery and strife that they had witnessed over the past couple of months, they were still looking forward to one of the most joyous times of the year.

But that's Bridget for you. She was an advocate for fellow evacuees, even though she was also in need. She was the strength that any man would look for in his mate, but she didn't have a problem with keeping her strength in its place and allowing Keith, to still know that she honored and respected him unconditionally.

It often cracked me up when we were talking and she'd stop and get clarification from him, "Keith, is that what they told us when we went there the other day?" "Keith, what was that number that they gave us again?" Keith this, Keith that and Keith forever I hope.

They are an outstanding couple and I pray that this experience has guaranteed longevity for their relationship, if that be what God wills.

"Yes, that would be awesome to include in the book. Look for that package no later than next week and it'll be self-addressed. All you'll have to do is drop it back in the mail to me once you've finished it."

We had closing comments and said our good-byes, with kind thoughts of our next conversation being greatly anticipated.

Bridget and Keith's Story

Shandra: Did you evacuate immediately?

Bridget: We evacuated on Sunday, the day before Katrina hit at around 11:30 a.m. The drive to Houston was over 12 hours long.

Shandra: What went through your mind when you did?

Bridget: My thoughts were that the hurricane would soon be over and that we would be returning home in about two days. Additionally, I felt that the trip was one well deserved, given our usual work schedule. I saw it as an opportunity for us to unwind and enjoy much needed rest. I said to myself, everything will be OK- no need to worry.

Shandra: How many are in your family?

Bridget: (8) My husband, our five children, a grandchild and myself.

Shandra: Did all of you make it out?

Bridget: We all made it out, but other close family members remained in what was thought to be very safe areas, in high-rise apartment buildings.

Shandra: Have you heard from other family members and loved ones who didn't travel with you?

Bridget: We heard from some other family members on the third day after Katrina, at around 8:30 a.m., when my sister, Kim, called me. We subsequently heard from other family members over an additional two-week period.

Shandra: What was life like for you before Katrina?

Bridget: We were striving to maintain our small business and to pay the mortgage on a home that we had purchased just three years earlier. We worked long hours and paid the bills, always determined to make ends meet and to stay on top of them. It was some times a struggle, but at least we had something to work with.

Shandra: What is it like as a result?

Bridget: We still feel the shock of it all. Our lives have changed tremendously. I lost my job as a manager at a group home; we lost the business that my husband struggled to build and maintain; we are no longer a family unit – some of our older children and other family members are scattered around the country. We all feel so displaced. One word that would really sum it up is – fragmented!! We fear a future that is yet uncertain. We wonder if our city, of New Orleans will ever reflect the uniqueness it is known for. That uniqueness is all of us…we blend together to make this place. It is the people, the way we talk, the way we walk, the way we second line, the way we party, the way we worship, the way we eat and the dishes we eat, the way we smile at strangers and each other, the conversation that no one else, but us really understand. It is the language, an expression, like no other!! If the real people are no longer a part of the fabric of this city, there is no New Orleans, as defined by us and as defined by the people who have visited New Orleans in the past, and have the experience of being amongst us.

Shandra: Are you currently in a shelter? If not, where do you reside?

Bridget: We are in our home. There was minimal damage, but we are in it and maintaining as best as we can.

Shandra: If they were to rebuild New Orleans successfully, would you go back? Why or why not?

Bridget: We are back in New Orleans and we will not allow anyone to keep us away. We are trying to rebuild this city, despite the many obstacles. We've demanded to play a role and have those who are native to New Orleans to be the ones to do the work. I was born and raised in New Orleans. My roots are here. There is no other place on the planet like my New Orleans!! I hope that all of my family members and friends will come back home. I am determined to continue work towards that end. My spirit has been weakened, but it hasn't been broken. There is too much at stake. I say, give us back our city!!

Shandra: What is it that you'd tell people about Hurricane Katrina and the way that things were handled by local, state and federal entities? Could it have been better?

Bridget: First of all, shockingly, our local administrators could not have understood the meaning of mandatory evacuation and the helplessness of so many of our elderly and disabled, who did not have the means nor the ability to leave their homes on their own. For many, a knock on the door and an offer to carry them off to safety would have resulted in a different outcome – many needlessly lost their lives.
Secondly, Federal, State, and Local officials all bear the responsibility for the shameful lack of response to the victims of this tragedy whom went without help for days and weeks on end. The suffering of thousands of African-Americans at the Super Dome and Convention Center in squalor conditions, without food or water and or basic hygiene needs.

This was shown around the world and it shamed the richest country in the world – The United States of America. One thing for sure, such a picture would not have existed had they been white!

Shandra: What is it that you'd like to share about this experience and where you are right now, emotionally, spiritually, etc?

Bridget: Be strong and keep the faith. It is by faith that we have come this far. God will work it all out.

Shandra: Any other closing comments you'd like to make?

Bridget: Only that we will rise again, we will become a better place in spite of all that seems to be working against us. Each day we get a little stronger and in that strength comes our will to remain undefeated with all that has happened. May God continue to bless those who suffered through Hurricanes Katrina and Rita, those who lost their lives, those who aided us, and those who sat and watched in horror as this played out before their eyes.

Since I was making my rounds, I decided to give Mary and Karl a call to see how things were going with them.

She had stepped out for a minute, but Karl and I chatted a while longer, before ending the call. He's a low-key, soft-spoken man. Although tall in physique and intimidating by sight, Karl is a gentle and deep thinking person who absorbs much of that around him.

At the shelter (where we all stayed during Rita), he was hardly present without Mary being close by. You could look at them and tell that they had a rather unique bond.

Nae-Nae and I liked them both immediately. Mary smiled non-stop and greeted all who crossed her path and that only drew you in more.

We'd sit and watch TV for a while and then get lost in a deep discussion about the impact of the hurricanes and they're being double evacuees.

Mary's way of expressing herself would have you hanging on to her every word. She'd lower her voice to a whisper and then bring it back up to deliver that last mouth-watering morsel for 'hungry' listeners.

When needed, Karl would chime in to validate what she had shared and would then nod his head, as to be certain that we knew what she was sharing was the absolute truth.

They were interviewed by a reporter from *USA Today*, and their story appeared in the September 26, 2005, edition of the paper, Section 4, first page.

When I called to let her know that I had gone online and read it, she was ecstatic. I told her how to go online and find it too, but she wasn't able to navigate it like she needed to, so I'll have to see if I can check the archives for it and obtain one for her. In the meantime, she said that she'd get in touch with the reporter and see if he'd get a back copy for them and send it.

When I made it in from my errands I saw that the message light was blinking and I went over to hear them. I was nearly jumping out of my skin when I realized that it was her.

I immediately called the number that she left in the message. She answered, but I had a 'senior moment.' I had forgotten who I called, and hoped she wouldn't notice. After a second or two of pausing from me, I was finally able to release a jubilant, "Hello Miss Mary! This is Shandra. I just got back in and got your call and I wanted to get right back to you. How are you doing?"

"Hello darling! We're fine, thanks. How are y'all doing?" she sounded just as happy to be hearing from me.

"I can't complain. We're hanging in there, thanks. I'm glad that I caught you. I originally called to see if you'd want to have your story told in the book that I'm currently working on, concerning Hurricanes Katrina and Rita. I met some wonderful people during those times and I'd like to make others aware of what things were like for all of you," I finished.

Being void of hesitance, she said, "I'd love to do it. Just tell me what you need and I'll do it. I don't mind helping you out at all. You and your baby made such an impression on me that I'd do anything that I could for you."

"Thank you so much Miss Mary, I really appreciate it. What I'll need is your mailing address to send it to. It's a questionnaire that you'll fill out and send back to me. I'll take care of the postage and that will make it that much easier for you to deal with. I'd also like a picture to use. Please don't hesitate to add to it, as you like. I only ask basic questions, but I want you to know that you have free reign in your responses. Is that OK?"

"Absolutely. Jot down my address and get it to me. As soon as I get it I can work on it and get it back to you. Shandra, I have to say that I'm enjoying myself now and in all my travels, I was always grateful for where I had been. I love New Orleans and the fact that I spent the better part of my life there, but there's nothing there for me now and the Lord doesn't have to send me too many signs before I take heed. I've been treated well here in Texas and I believe that He had a divine purpose in my landing here. I have nothing bad to say about anything and I'm going to be glad that I'm even alive to be able to say that. Many weren't as fortunate and *that's* why I can still be happy," she reflected.

Our call would end with me telling her to look for the package and promises of our getting together real soon. It was quite refreshing knowing that we'd have that chance again.

Mary and Karl's Story

Shandra: Did you evacuate immediately?

Mary: No. I really had plans to ride the storm out at home. Mandatory evacuation orders (by city and state officials) were the reason that I eventually left. I couldn't convince my son, Karl to leave with me though. I left the city that Sunday morning with tears in my eyes, convinced that I would never see my son *alive* again.

Shandra: What went through your mind when you did?

Mary: My daughter, Dianna and I hurriedly left New Orleans. I packed nothing but the basics, underwear, toothbrush/toothpaste, etc. As I put my small bag into the car, I turned and went back into the house to once again try and convince Karl to come too. He remained calm and assured me that he would be OK. At this point I was left believing that he was ready to die. I went ahead and left, being sure to ask God to spare his life.

Shandra: How many are in your family?

Mary: There are five in my family. There are two girls, two boys and myself.

Shandra: Did all of you make it out?

Mary: Yes, we all made it out and our children and grandchildren also. There are seven of them, two grand daughters and five grand sons. We are all scattered, but safe. Thank God.

Shandra: Have you heard from other family members and loved ones who didn't travel with you?

Mary: Yes. All of my family members are scattered from Washington D.C. to Baton Rouge, LA and I have spoken with my other son who at present is in Arlington, Texas. I've heard from my daughters in Baton Rouge, LA and Jacksonville, Florida. I thank God that all are well.

Shandra: What was life like for you before Katrina?

Mary: I was really a laid back senior, enjoying life. I worked part-time and always looked forward to traveling with my sorority sisters. We traveled to conventions every year. Last year we went to New York City and everyone had a lovely time there. Every day I looked forward to going to work and being able to help seniors and disabled people. It was a real joy. I had a pretty handsome wardrobe, dressed well, kept on top of things concerning my health and basically began to realize that life was mellowing out for me. I had less worry, less stress, and a lovely townhouse. My son, who was a truck driver, he lived with me when he was not on the road. My past time was church every Sunday and to work some hours five days a week. My key thoughts were to stay busy, help someone else and live and let live.

Shandra: What is it like as a result?

Mary: I've learned to never take things for granted, no matter what your situation is. I can only say this, I had the notion that Katrina would produce flooding and high winds, but never did I believe life would have had such a drastic change. I now know what it's like to have and I know what it's like to not have. What a difference a day made. All of this is the result of Katrina. Not forgetting that Rita caused my son and me to end up sleeping in our car when we were on our way to College Station, Texas. A police officer saw us and directed us to a shelter. We thank God for those two police officers. They demonstrated love and care to perfect strangers. They will never be forgotten.

Shandra: Are you currently in a shelter? If not, where do you reside?

Mary: No, I reside in a lovely apartment in College Station, Texas. It's going to take time to get on my feet, but I've learned to take it one step at a time and have patience.

Shandra: If they were to rebuild New Orleans successfully, would you go back? Why or why not?

Mary: No, I had planned to relocate to Mississippi. But things happened while I was in Mississippi that made me have a change of heart. The city was not too commercialized. There was no bus service or other conveniences I was used to having. I've always had a fear of New Orleans sinking. I even had nightmares about it. This was the best time to leave and I'm happy in my new residence, with no regrets of leaving New Orleans.

Shandra: What is it that you'd tell people about Hurricane Katrina and the way that things were handled by local, state and federal entities? Could it have been better?

Mary: Yes, there comes a time when emergencies occur and the red tape can be chaos, while you are displaced, with no food, clothes or shelter. It can also put you at odds with your political leaders. You should always have a plan if you need to make a sudden move and not have to wait on local and state officials to say that you must go or stay. This has really been a learning experience for my entire family.

Shandra: What is it that you'd like to share about this experience and where you are right now, emotionally, spiritually, etc?

Mary: This experience has allowed me to see a change in my son Karl, who expressed what fear he had and how sorry he was for not leaving with me the day that my daughter and I left. He is more humble. My other son, Clarence, who I hadn't seen since Katrina and Rita hit, was able to come down with his family and visit me. I feel so much relief. I just didn't know I could feel so happy. Only God could give me this kind of peace. I only miss one thing from New Orleans, my church pastor and other Christian sisters and brothers.

Shandra: Any other closing comments you'd like to make?

Mary: I was in a shelter in Houston, Texas and had the pleasure of meeting some wonderful people. Ms. Shandra and her daughter Nae-Nae had a profound effect on me, one that's never going to be forgotten. I ask God to bless her and her daughters. I love them all. All of this was the result of Rita.

Miss Harriet is a seasoned, outspoken and determined woman who I met when I was with Theresa at a Wal-Mart store.

She was gliding around in her scooter and asked me if I knew how she could catch a cab. "Ma'am, from what I've seen, cabs don't really run out this way on an every hour, several times a day schedule. If you go to the customer service desk they should be able to help you to get one. I don't know how long it'll take, but I do see them out here on occasion."

She turned it around and went back into the store. We continued to wait for Theresa's son. They had gone in and found some really nice things and decided to get them, but there wasn't enough room in my car to carry it all.

When Miss Harriet returned Theresa looked at her for a while longer and then asked, "Aren't you from New Orleans Parish?" Miss Harriet perked up, almost shocked and noticeably eager to see who it was who seemed to recognize her.

"Yes, I lived there. You know me?" she asked. Theresa smiled and said, "Yes, you and your daughter used to go through the area. Y'all are Jehovah's Witnesses, right? You live in that big pretty house on that hill."

Miss Harriet smiled and nodded her head. Theresa's next question would get an answer that surprised us all. "Where's your daughter? Is she here with you?" Miss Harriet closed her eyes, shook her head and answered, "Naw, she had to get back there to work. Her area wasn't hit and she helped me to get out of there."

Although we were surprised that she was in a strange city, alone, we didn't add to the already tense moment. I started reaching into my purse and said, "Well, we can't have that. You might *be* here alone, but we aren't going to allow you to *stay* here alone. Where are you staying? Give me information on how I can contact you and we'll be sure to keep you in the presence of others and feeling that you have someone here to deal with."

She perked up a bit and said, "OK, that would be nice. I don't know nobody baby. I'm over here at the LaQuinta. My room number is one-oh-five. I need to get in touch with the Red Cross and FEMA. I don't know what I can get. Have y'all got anything yet?"

I smiled at her and said, "I live here. I'm a Disaster Relief Volunteer who has been assisting them. That was why I also told you that we weren't going to let you be here all by yourself."

She looked at each of us, almost like she was tattooing our faces in her memory. "OK, I appreciate that baby. I don't go out of my room or do too much because I don't know anybody."

I placed my hand on her shoulder and replied, "Well, you do now. We'll be calling and checking on you frequently."

As if it were meant to be, Theresa's son arrived at the store within a few minutes of the taxi. I was able to watch her load up before we pulled off.

As promised, I called and checked on her as much as possible and offered as much of myself as I could. She was able to get back to New Orleans to retrieve some of her personal belongings.

She had beautiful clothes and jewelry. Although some of it was costume jewelry, she was still a class act. It was evident in the pictures that she showed of her home.

My mouth literally dropped open when she showed me before and after pictures of it. Shucks, I hurt for her. The furniture was the elegantly designed, Eighteenth Century looking pieces.

There was a mesmerizing statue that sat almost in the middle of the floor. The dining room table was set with the finest of dishes and flatware.

The rings that held the napkins in place looked as if craftsmen from another era had taken each and every one of them and created the perfect design.

She lost more than anyone could ever be able to calculate, but regardless of that, she maintained her poise and dignity.

She was anxious to get out of the hotel room. She had been there for two months and it was wearing thin on her patience.

She had no refrigerator, no stove and no real meals, since she wasn't able to prepare them herself and save them, she had to keep buying fast food or meals good for one day.

I looked into apartments for her, but the ones that were accepting the vouchers that FEMA or the Red Cross, were providing, were quickly at capacity and had already started waiting lists.

I offered to let her stay with me, but I live upstairs and she is not able to climb them. Nonetheless, the journey was to be had and we were quite prepared for the trip.

She had missed September and October's Social Security checks and the fact that she was getting no mail at all concerned me.

It doesn't take two months for mail to be redirected, especially if some of it is local. I told her that I'd be more than happy to let her use my post office box if she was that concerned about it.

After several more days and money on hand coming down to just a few dollars, we did change her mail from the hotel to my P.O. Box.

I was floored when she started receiving mail at my box in a week's time. I didn't like what that was making me think about the people at the hotel.

It doesn't matter that I thought it because Miss Harriet had no trouble voicing that she was wondering whether they were returning her mail so that her aid would be held up and cause her to have to stay in the room that much longer.

A longer stay in the room meant more money for them and a hotel that was at capacity would most definitely be raking in some good federal dollars.

It's sad that we had to think this way, but her daughter would report to her that some truck rental companies were charging as much as $900 for some of their trucks.

Not to mention that apartments that used to rent for four or five hundred dollars were well past the thousand-dollar mark.

It's shameful the way that people used this time to fleece taxpayers and these people who were in dire need of help. What was it that the O'Jays said in one of their songs? "For a small piece of paper, it sure carries a lot of weight."

Harriett's Story

I would interview Miss Harriett on November 19, 2005. This would be my second spiritual blessing for this particular weekend.

I hadn't heard from her for about two weeks and I was a bit concerned because she never lets a long time pass before we speak on the phone.

This was the case with Theresa and me, too. She was missing in action for about three weeks and calls were going unanswered or returned.

Finally on Friday she called and let me know that she was given the opportunity to go back to New Orleans to retrieve some of her belongings, if they were salvageable, and she jumped on it.

Miss Harriet had taken a trip back home too and came back with many bags of her clothes. She had washed and sent them to the cleaners.

They were hanging about the room and jewelry was spread across the bed in a box, some was lying on the table near the phone.

I had just picked Nae-Nae up from work and called to be sure that she was awake and ready for me to drop the permission form off to her.

She asked me to fax papers to FEMA. They had announced that no more payments would be made to hotels and motels that were housing evacuees, so she was a bit anxious about that.

After going to the office and seeing that the guest services representative got them faxed, I went back to the room and let her know that I was going to be leaving.

I handed her the papers that I brought and she said, "Can't you just ask me and I tell you while you write it down?" Nae-Nae was tired and I really wanted to get going, but it would be better for me to go ahead and get Miss Harriett's story as soon as I could.

I looked over at Nae-Nae and she smiled, letting me know that she'd be OK if I went ahead and interviewed her.

I sat back down and got comfortable. I barely had my pen poised to write when she asked, "You know that Time is releasing a book or something about Hurricane Katrina, don't you?"

I looked up at her and replied, "No, I wasn't aware of that." She frowned a little and said, "Don't you watch the news? They had it on there the other day."

I smiled and said, "I must have missed it, but no, I don't watch TV that much these days." I wasn't going to tell her that coverage of Katrina had pretty much zapped me of any interest in the news. I just let it be and got down to the business of asking her the questions about her ordeal.

Shandra: Did you evacuate immediately?

Harriet: Yes, I left on the 27th of August and ended up in Baytown, Texas.

Shandra: What went through your mind when you did?

Harriet: I was thinking that it would hit and be over with, but I wanted to obey evacuation orders and warnings. I really thought I'd have a little vacation and it be back to normal in a day or two. (She invites Nae-Nae to crawl up on the bed next to her and tells her to grab a pillow off of the other bed).

Shandra: How many are in your family?

Harriet: Just me, I lived alone on the East bank.

Shandra: Did all of you make it out?

Harriet: Yes, me, my daughter and her two daughters left together, but she returned because her area wasn't affected much by it. She lived on the West Bank.

Shandra: Have you heard from other family members and loved ones who didn't travel with you?

Harriet: Yes, all of them. I heard from my last grandson yesterday. He's in San Antonio, Texas. (She's proud of the personal items that she was able to salvage and invites me over to look at some of her jewelry that was in the pawnshop. I'm in utter amazement at these pieces of jewelry. The rings, necklaces and bracelets are exquisitely adorned with various jewels and charms. She gives a brief history of where she got them and how one of the diamonds conveniently came out while she had them in the pawnshop. After a few more minutes of her talking about them and how she liked to wear them, we got back to the questions).

Shandra: What was life like for you before Katrina?

Harriet: It was good for me, but I don't know if you want to say this, but after the O. J. Simpson verdict, it seemed that blacks were treated badly in New Orleans. I don't know whether or not he did it, but it was very noticeable to me. I also believe that there was something to reports about the levee being blown up. I'm suspicious of them now and I wonder what has happened to all of the money that they say was raised. I was supposed to get two thousand dollars and I'm still waiting on it. I'm going to tell my daughter and tell her that I believe I'm going to make this my home. They're crooked people. I call the French Quarter Sodom and Gomorrah and the other part is Blood on the Moon. They intentionally let that water loose on us and I can't stand knowing how they did us.

Shandra: Miss Harriett, this is the story of Hurricanes Katrina and Rita evacuees and what *you* tell me is what I'm going to write. I don't care who has a problem with it because it isn't about them it's about y'all. Feel free to tell me what you will. I have no problem writing it as you tell it. I owe *them* nothing. Next question, what is it like as a result?

Harriet: I'm very confused and afraid of all that has happened. I don't trust anyone or what they tell me. It'll be hard for me to. I don't guess anyone would ever be able to know what this has done to us. (She points to some pictures that are on the table. She explains that the two females are her daughters. An old 60's looking picture is of her son that was killed in a car wreck over twenty years ago. One of the pictures of her daughter is smeared and somewhat discolored.

She shares that she pulled it out of a pile of water and slushy goo and cleaned it up as best as she could. I look into her soft, yet disturbed eyes and know that this won't be something that she will easily forget. Again, the questions).

Shandra: Are you currently in a shelter? If not, where do you reside?

Harriet: No. I'm staying in a hotel, but an apartment should be ready for me sometime next week.

Shandra: If they were to rebuild New Orleans successfully, would you go back? Why or why not?

Harriet: I don't think so because I'd always be afraid to go to sleep because I'd be thinking that the water was going to come and drown me as I slept. It stinks and I can't trust the water. You know those restaurants and things are open and I'm trying to figure out how people are eating in them when the water has been so bad and the stench unbearable. I know you have to eat and live, but that seems to be too much right now. They'll never build the levee to handle the highest level of hurricane and I don't want to chance it. The political aspect of New Orleans is corrupt and I'm basically confused with it all. I'll never eat another piece of seafood from there. The coroner has five hundred bodies that he can't identify and many more are in the homes in the Ninth Ward. That's how they found my next-door neighbor. She was asleep when Katrina hit and her body had floated near the door. It was a month before they found her. I don't care what they say, they still haven't found all of those bodies and they aren't going to give a true count of them when they do.

Shandra: What is it that you'd tell people about Hurricane Katrina and the way that things were handled by local, state and federal entities? Could it have been better?

Harriet: I'd really like to say that it was drastically mishandled. They're asking us out of the rooms already and we have nothing. You could answer that by looking at the news and seeing all that they are saying about this and how the officials didn't do what they were supposed to. Governor Blanco will go down in history as the worst Governor ever. While Katrina will go down as one of the worst natural disasters. We're nothing, we have nothing, and we lost everything. They don't want us back. Things that we used to pay a dollar for are now five dollars. They've made everything unreachable for us. (Nae-Nae started snoring at this point. I instructed Miss Harriett to pop her upside the head. She refused, saying that she liked to hear people snore because it put her to sleep as well. Nae-Nae heard us talking about her, awoke and apologized for her slight. Miss Harriett wouldn't hear of it and told her to go back to sleep if she wanted to).

Shandra: What is it that you'd like to share about this experience and where you are right now, emotionally, spiritually, etc?

Harriet: I was very emotionally disturbed when I walked in and saw the condition of my home. My faith in God and all that He's been to me are what has sustained me. I'm a crippled, elderly woman who can't swim and this did a lot to me, but I know that I'll be OK. I don't want to look back though. I want to look forward. I want to try and forget. I don't want to dwell on what was allowed to happen to us.

Shandra: Any other closing comments you'd like to make?

Harriet: Yes, I hope that this is a way for others to know that God is speaking to us in his own way and is trying to pull us closer to him. Time is drawing to a close and we need to be ready. We should all pay attention to the signs. Can everyone else see them?

She appeared to be sleepy.
I kissed her on the cheek and Nae-Nae and I saw our way out, securing the door behind us.

Although it isn't uncommon for us to get visitors at church, there was something obviously 'interesting' about a couple who came to church two weeks after Rita.

She was a quiet woman with a beautiful smile. Her spirit projected hints of devotion to her husband and total submission to God.

They came with two young men who turned out to be their sons. They were somewhat shy acting, but that all faded once they were asked to honor us with a song.

They went up, one singing while playing the organ and the other played the drums. In no time at all, they had the church rejoicing in grand style. They did a beautiful number that left the church electrified.

However, by the time the father had finished his testimony of how they were plucked from the roof of a building, after flooding drove them there, the saints were rejoicing. The ordeal of how they continued to move from one floor to a higher one (as they noticed water coming into the building) was gripping and kept us hanging onto his every word.

He was a small, fast moving, fast-talking, lively gentleman. His comments were humorous and spellbinding. It was hard to tell that he had been through anything remotely close to disaster, his spirit said otherwise.

Most of us shook our heads or uttered, "Lord have mercy," whenever he'd share something that was too incredible for us to imagine.

Looking at this family was absolute proof that God had to be the head of their lives because through it all, they still managed to sing, they still managed to shout out in victory and they continuously lifted up praises at how they got over.

Isaiah and Deborah Johnson's Story

Shandra: Did you evacuate immediately?

Deborah: No, we did not evacuate immediately. We did not feel the need to leave and go out of town because we were going into a 'hurricane proof' facility. We evacuated because of the rising water and not so much because of the hurricane itself. We were later evacuated by helicopter from the roof of the building that we had sought refuge in.

Shandra: What went through your mind when you did?

Deborah: We knew that God was in control, no matter what, and we were going to leave all in His capable hands. It caused some anxious moments, but we kept our faith in God and knew that His will would be done.

Shandra: How many are in your family?

Deborah: There are four of us. My husband, Isaiah, my sons Derrick and Chris, and then me.

Shandra: Did all of you make it out?

Deborah: Yes we did.

Shandra: Have you heard from other family members and loved ones who didn't travel with you?

Deborah: Yes, we didn't have a problem with communication. We were able to speak to those who we needed to.

Shandra: What was life like for you before Katrina?

Deborah: Life was 'normal,' comfortable and very peaceful. We lived in a nice neighborhood and we had a very good church family. My husband had a job and I owned my own business. My sons were working and life was good for us.

Shandra: What is it like as a result?

Deborah: Initially, it was very difficult coping with the change, but as the days, weeks and months have gone by, the Lord has blessed us tremendously. We've lost much and have been blessed with replacements of that which we lost.

Shandra: Are you currently in a shelter? If not, where do you reside?

Deborah: No, we are not in a shelter. We currently have a home in Spring, Texas.

Shandra: If they were to rebuild New Orleans successfully, would you go back? Why or why not?

Deborah: If they were to rebuild New Orleans successfully, I would not go back because I believe this is where the Lord would have my family and me. This has been a change for the better for all of us and God is *in* it.

Shandra: What is it that you'd tell people about Hurricane Katrina and the way that things were handled by local, state and federal entities? Could it have been better?

Deborah: Hurricane Katrina was one of the worst storms that we have ever experienced in our lives, thus far. It also sent a message that man's way in the absence of God brings displeasure to Him and eventually His wrath will come. Now as far as the way things were handled, I believe that for the most part our rescue was carried out with care and compassion. Bus loading was chaotic and there was a lack of compassion by those in charge. It could have been organized better to make the difficult situation a little more bearable. We waited on the side of a highway for days to be rescued so it was a trying time for everyone. When we were lifted from the building, as the water rose to cover it, I shuddered at the sight of the dark, murky water that washed away many lives.

Shandra: What is it that you'd like to share about this experience and where you are right now, emotionally, spiritually, etc?

Deborah: I would like to share that having Christ in our lives before the tragedy occurred made all the difference in the world. There is NOTHING that God cannot sustain us through. He has proven to be the God that we needed Him to be. Also, in keeping our eyes on Him, we were able to see that the experience of the storm was a good thing. It showed us that, whatever He started in us, He would complete. Emotionally we are doing well and are stable. Spiritually, our lives continue, day by day. We have been blessed to have a Pastor and First Lady – Superintendent Eddie Toppen, Jr. and Mattie Toppen, who have fed our souls with the Word of God and much love. God knew what He was doing for us. Life has resumed and we have more now than we did before. We also have a loving church family to have their arms wide open from the very first time that we came.

Shandra: Any other closing comments you'd like to make?

Deborah: I count it a privilege to be able to voice in writing and recall where the Lord has brought us from, up to this time. We are indeed thankful.

My niece Brenda was in route to Houston, when Rita began to close in on us. She lived in Beaumont, Texas and did not want to take the chance of being unable to get out, once she struck.

As things got worse and I seriously began to consider getting Nae-Nae to a safer place, I was sure to tell her to get to Houston as best as she could and when she did I'd send Nae-Nae with her. With each call that she made, I would become just a little more anxious.

Thursday would come and go with me hearing nothing more from her, but plenty from Nita who was in constant contact with me and wondering if I had heard anything.

They were getting hit and miss messages from her, but not enough information to let me know an exact location or time of arrival.

When Friday came and we learned that she had been re-routed to St. Augustine, Texas, we were spent. I had no idea where that was or how she would get from there.

Furthermore, it left me in a tight spot because I didn't know what Nae-Nae and I would do. I didn't know if that meant she was still going to try and come to Houston or if it meant that she would stay there until it blew over.

All I knew was that she had made it out of Beaumont with some friends of hers and would be trying to get in touch with me.

Whatever the case may be, I wasn't going to leave her unless I knew for sure that she wasn't coming. I would have never lived it down had I left home and she came here looking for me. Especially if something were to happen to her or one of the children.

As it turned out, my sister Liz, who lives in Plano, Texas, went and got her and my brothers drove down and picked her up from there. I was quite relieved when I knew that she was with family again.

I myself had been snatched up at the last minute and able to go and stay at a Red Cross shelter, so all was well for the time being.

As is a part of history now, Rita made a last minute turn and hit the Beaumont and Port Arthur areas the hardest. Houston had dodged a bullet and was able to breathe a sigh of relief.

Brenda would land a job and find an apartment fairly soon after relocating to Oklahoma and she was fine with her decision to not go back to Beaumont immediately.

She was an intake representative assisting Katrina and Rita evacuees who were attempting to receive HUD or FEMA assistance. She told me of a case where a young woman was pregnant and had been rescued from Hurricane Katrina by her father, who lived in Baton Rouge, Louisiana.

Only two days after going to get her, he was struck and killed by a car, while on his way into his place of employment.

Not only was she left fatherless, but she also became homeless, as she would have nowhere to go after having the baby. She was not employed, had no income and would not be able to keep up the taxes and other expenses associated with the house.

She shared how she was left in tears and crying with this young lady who also went on to explain that the baby's father was killed in the hell that Katrina unleashed.

All I could do was shake my head. I could find no words to relay the level of shock or disbelief that I was experiencing.

Brenda had no recollection of where the mother of this young lady was, but she did briefly mention a few 'estranged' family members.

I asked her to pass my information along to her should she get the opportunity to speak with her again.

If she needed to get out of Baton Rouge and we could get her to Houston, I'd get her a place to stay. Especially with a baby who was due November 1, 2005.

Although I had been putting up a good front, dealing with the Katrina and Rita evacuees was beginning to take its toll on me.

The grim reports and constant pictures of survivors running into the arms of celebrities like Oprah Winfrey, Chris Rock, Jamie Foxx and T. D. Jakes were indicative of the despair that followed Katrina. How crippling for Rita to come along and dismantle everything that was developing with Katrina relief efforts.

Brenda's Story

Shandra: Did you evacuate immediately?

Brenda: Yes, as fast as circumstances would allow me to. We packed the night before and the next morning my Aunt Nita called and told me to watch the news. It was about 5:30 a.m. We were asked to leave, but I wasn't able to leave right away. We were all very nervous and wanting to be on the road as soon as possible, but it wasn't happening quite as I hoped it would.

Shandra: What went through your mind when you did?

Brenda: The first thing was that my children would remain with me and continue to be safe. I had heard about the traffic and people who were being overcome by the heat, not to mention overheating cars and the bumper-to-bumper traffic jams. All of the frustrations that were being shown on the news were scary. I didn't know where we'd end up or whether we'd beat Hurricane Rita.

Shandra: How many are in your family?

Brenda: There are four of us. Derrick is 8, Destiny is 5, Brendien is 4 and then there's me.

Shandra: Did all of you make it out?

Brenda: Yes we did, thank God.

Shandra: Have you heard from other family members or loved ones that didn't travel with you?

Brenda: Yes, I heard from my mother, who stayed in Beaumont, TX during the hurricane, she's OK. My sister went to Louisiana at first, but ended up in a shelter in San Antonio. She now has an apartment and has chosen to remain in Houston.

Shandra: What was life like for you before Hurricane Rita?

Brenda: To be honest with you, it wasn't as nice as I would have liked it. I was alone, raising my children and my mother and sister and I didn't see each other on a regular basis and it was sometimes overwhelming.

Shandra: What is it like as a result?

Brenda: It's somewhat better. I'm in a better place and I have accomplished much. I see family members on a regular basis. I have peace of mind and being with this many family members gives me an assurance that all will be OK, no matter what might happen. They're throwed off, but for the most part I'm hearing from them or seeing them every day. I really enjoy being with my Grandmother again. She is a mess! Gone "Big Mama!"

Shandra: Are you currently in a shelter? If not, where do you reside?

Brenda: No, I currently have my own apartment and when I was relocated (after getting out of Beaumont), my Aunt Liz came and got me. I have been with family every since, up until the time that I got my own apartment.

Shandra: If they were to rebuild your section of Beaumont successfully, would you go back? Why or why not?

Brenda: No, I would not. I don't want to deal with the emotional aspect of returning there and what added to my unhappiness, even before the storm.

Shandra: What is it that you'd tell people about Hurricane Rita and the way that things were handled by local, state and federal entities? Could it have been better?

Brenda: Yes, it could have been better. They didn't seem to be prepared for Rita victims and they saw Katrina evacuees in a different light. They seemed to overlook others who suffered through Rita. I don't mean to say that Rita was as deadly or destructive as Katrina, but the response and the still waiting was as evident for Rita evacuees as it was for Katrina, the fatality rate was just a lot different.

Shandra: What is it that you'd like to share about this experience and where you are right now, emotionally spiritually?

Brenda: Right now I can pretty much say that I'm fine. My children are being taken care of and many burdens have been lifted. Everything is fresh and new. I'm happy and remain focused on what I'm trying to accomplish. I'm continuously working on self and life can only get better from this point on. God will order my steps.

Shandra: Any other closing comments you'd like to make?

Brenda: I pray that anyone who was caught up in either of these two hurricanes (Katrina and Rita) have settled down and are receiving some sense of stability. I pray that they maintain the strength to keep it behind them and will walk away still counted among the "survivors."

Storm Warning

No peace could prepare us for the force of your strike
No calm could console us as we fought to sustain life
No one could ever imagine what it was like in our shoes
No truth was ever slanted as was reported in the news

What nation would allow citizens of its own to linger?
What dare we think of the anguish that this did bring her?
What say you to the lives that were lost?
What can be done to rectify this shameful cost?

Oh what terror your vast waters did bring
Oh sorrow and despair have been your offspring
Oh God of Mercy, God of Compassion
Oh people of America will we ever become one

We'll roll with this punch and prepare to dodge others
We'll reach out freely to each of our brothers
We'll remember the ones who perished in the water's rage
We'll admonish the 'slow calls' that higher ups made

Let us not walk away unprepared to live this down
Let us bring forth the positives; allow peace to be found
Let every man, woman and child awake each morning
With the painful reminder of this storm warning

My Rant

I've presented these stories, my story, their stories, our stories, in hopes that others would have a better idea of who was affected by Hurricanes Katrina and Rita.

I felt it was important to know this because had some in the media had their way, *all* of the evacuees would be illiterate thugs, welfare recipients, ingrates or other plagues upon society.

Nothing could be farther from the truth. It has been my experience that many of these people were decent, law-abiding homeowners, business owners, retirees, homemakers, former service men and women and other responsible citizens of this great land.

To have sidestepped them, to give way to trashy and jaded journalism should be considered a slight on all of us who know better.

Any city, town or state can have their share of 'undesirables,' but to make it appear that most of them lived in New Orleans was a shameful and low blow.

I've always been one to "call it as I see it" and this time it takes the cake. I pray that many more will take a stand against this kind of journalism and defamation of any and all people of any given ethnic background.

For too long the powers that be have been allowed to shovel their propaganda down our throats and many of us swallowed, without so much as asking for a glass of water to help it go down.

I'm not some militant crackpot who wants to overthrow the government or otherwise see blood shed to get better leaders, but it would do my heart glad to see someone stand up, look them square in the eye and say "Not today. We've had enough and you *will* become more accountable. You *will* do as the people wish and you *will* deliver to me honest, accurate and unbiased accounts of events that have affected us all."

Again, I'm not a member of any anti-government group nor do I have any agenda other than urging people to stop accepting any and everything that is thrown their way and to take a stand for what they know to be 'right.'

Too many have fought and died for you to have the most basic of freedoms and you still won't exercise your right to be heard concerning them.

Although it's nice to know that they aren't afraid to speak out, it shouldn't take Oprah Winfrey, Kanye West, Jamie Foxx, Danny Glover, Whoopi Goldberg, Bill Cosby, Dick Gregory and the many, many others who have done so, to be the first to speak out against the ills of society.

It's a given that they are "celebrities" who have amassed great wealth and can afford to stray from the mainstream norms of society, but John and Mary Q Citizen are just as qualified and believable.

In the weeks and months to follow Hurricane Katrina, her evacuees seemed to be making the news on a daily basis. There were three who were arrested for the murder of an elderly woman who took them in and there were others who were shot or stabbed to death in other acts of violence.

The crime rate is said to have soared since their arrival and the friction between the children in school has reached riot proportions, in some instances.

There's no doubt in my mind that the trauma from having lived this ordeal and their feelings of abandonment have been contributing factors with much of this, but we have to not let it keep us from making a commitment to continue to see them through this.

We are their "keeper." Anything that we can be caught doing to assist them in rebuilding their lives is our duty.

Know that there's another *storm* coming. Are you prepared for *it*?

Epilogue

In the months that have followed the devastation of Hurricanes Katrina and Rita, I have witnessed first hand how it has weighed in on life for some of those evacuees.

Some are content and determined to make the best of the new places that they now have to call "home," while others have shut down, are withdrawn and focus solely on being able to return to New Orleans.

I have since lost contact with a few of them and pray that all is well. I have no way of knowing whether they remain in Houston or have filtered back to parts of Louisiana, but wherever they may be, I am eternally grateful for them allowing me to tap into their innermost thoughts and feelings.

By one means or another, I'm in constant contact with those who are specifically named in the book. Without their cooperation none of this would have been made possible.

Mary Jones, while traveling to New Orleans to recover some of her goods, was able to come up after Christmas and spent the day with me. She looks great. She has a beautiful head of soft, curly hair. The gray accentuates it perfectly and brings out the more seasoned and gentle aspect of her character.

We started at the IHOP at SH 290 and Highway 6. I met her there and was going to lead her to my home so she could park her car and I take her to the bus station from there. We had a really pleasant lunch. She kept trying to pay for the tab and was disappointed when I wouldn't let her.

She was able to meet my oldest daughter, Bianca, and I shared with her pictures of my aunt and little sister, both passed away within fifty-two days of each other.

I had given her a copy of the book detailing my fight with Clinical Depression after losing them and she was quite pleased to finally lay eyes on the two whom I had drawn much of my strength from (outside of my mother).

When she saw the picture of my mother, she looked back at it and then at me. Her jaw dropped and she was at a loss for words. When she did finally speak she said, "Shandra! She looks just like my mother! My mother looks like that. I can't believe the resemblance."

I smiled at her and looked at the picture of my mother and went from her eyes, nose, mouth and general facial features to follow as she made comparisons to her mother's.

I enjoyed our time immensely and our trek to the bus station was one that we're sure to never forget. There were many people headed to New Orleans this night and from the overheard conversations and sounds of excitement in their voices, some of the post Christmas travelers wouldn't have it any other way.

She made her trip to New Orleans, got back to me safely and after packing her car up and getting on the road, she made it back home.

I would also go by and check on Miss Harriett. Her son and his wife were visiting for the holidays, so it was a pleasure to meet them. She had made fresh pots of red beans and rice and had her daughter-in-law to make me a bowl.

We touched base on all that seemed to be coming about with stories of evacuees in the news and how some of them seemed to be on 'self destructive' courses.

It has been reaching scary proportions and we wondered why it wasn't being made known that counseling had been set up and was available for those in need.

A Katrina evacuee was killed at a hotel in Houston on Thursday, December 29, 2005 and on Friday, December 30, 2005, there were four people shot when tensions between New Orleans evacuees and Houston apartment tenants escalated an already brewing "turf war."

This was only days after police in New Orleans shot and killed a man armed with a knife. I don't know what it would take for a happy medium to be reached, but it's truly a tragic footnote to an already devastating situation.

I wanted to be mindful of their time together so I said my "goodbye" and headed for home. It was good for me to have found her and make contact again.

She had lost her phone book that had my information in it and I had to find her based on the description of the apartment complex, located in a certain area. She took my information again and reminded me to not be a stranger.

I was on the phone with Teresa on New Year's Eve and she had been able to get a visit in with friends and family in Mississippi.

They had a wonderful Christmas and she was looking forward to the promises of 2006. Our cell signals were cut short and we ended with safe wishes and claims of moving forward with no obstacles from this point on.

I saw Isaiah and Deborah Johnson at church New Year's Eve and every Sunday that we are there, so I'll see and be in contact with them much.

Their sons, Derrick and Chris are blessings to the church, with their music and bubbly personalities. It is my hope that the closing of Katrina and the opening of a brand new start, in a brand new year, are written in ink on God's agenda for them.

My niece is doing well and is thoroughly enjoying the comforts of being with her father and my other siblings and their families.

It goes without saying that being with my mother again is a definite perk for remaining there. She's being told that she's a lot like me and I laugh as they continue to give some of the nieces to me.

Don't get me wrong, I'll gladly take them, but ummm… it's sometimes being said when they are sometimes being "bad." Need I say more?

Bridget and Keith Cloud are doing well and they became the grandparents of an adorable baby girl in early December. They are busy with getting their lives back on track and recovering fully from Katrina's blow.

As for me, I'm putting the finishing touches on four other novels. I will be rushing them to press as soon as I can slow down long enough to take in all that the whirlwind of the past few months has cast me in.

If you've never had a reason to *believe*, I ask you to find one now. God Bless You.

I Come As I Am

"My character and good name are all that I have, if altering either is a requirement for you to accept or acknowledge me, let me quietly remove myself from your sight, I will *not* conform."

Autograph Page

"Literary Angels"

Many thanks to the following patrons who were all too willing to see this book brought to fruition. Greater New Solomon Temple – COGIC, "Thank you!"

J. R. Parker
Liz and Leroy Williams
Benita Turner
Juli McKinney
Horace and Patricia Stewart
Supt. Eddie Toppen, Jr., and Mattie
Michael Landry and Family
Carlos and Samenta Willis
James and Deborah Edwards
Michael and Cathyrine Richardson
Gerald Hill
Marie Latin
David and Annette Porter
Alterman Sauls
Tom Weinkauf
Sheila Holt and Family
Kimberly Morrison
Carl Wilson and Family
Jean Green
Brenda Curtis
Arnetria "Smokie" Williams
Tina Moten
Jasmine Cade
Trenika Curtis
Monique Edwards
Gwendolyn "Nissie" Landry

Kristi "Blue" Landry
Arthur Curtis – Innovative Videos
Helen Thomas
Johnny Stewart
Annie Woods
Yevernett Anderson
Sharon Simpson
Sandra Batiste and Family
Therman and Debra Lamb
Frank Cottrell and Family
Clara Edwards and Family
Laura Solomon
The Lewis Family
Donna Blake
Darrell Hutton
Cheryl Rodgers and Family
Nicole Benn
Chanel Talbert
Paris Fitzgerald
Latonia Galberth
Becky Moore
Eric and Tasha Douglas
Atria Ealy and Family
Reva and Neva McClain
Mary Ellis
Sharon Thomas
Bryn Robinson

Updates

An article in today's *Houston Chronicle* (March 14, 2006) tragically drew to a close the life of Tyeisha Martin, a 19-yarold Katrina evacuee who was found slain in a surrounding county, last week.

Back in December, *Seventeen* magazine shared her story of survival with the world and today, her story of a life cut short will forever haunt us. How will this be explained to her 2-year-old daughter? Who will help her understand?

Also in this article was the fact that over two-dozen Louisiana evacuees were involved in a violent death in the greater Houston area.

Houston police report that as many as twenty-nine evacuees have been either victims or suspects in homicide cases and as of Monday (March 13, 2006), no new statistics were available.

On Saturday, March 11, 2006, William Petty, a 29-year-old Katrina evacuee was shot and killed by a Houston police officer after he answered the door of his apartment "armed" with a gun.

Police were following up on complaints that drug transactions were going on at the residence. After his death, it was determined that the gun in his possession was a toy.

On Monday, March 13, 2006, a Katrina evacuee was arrested in New Orleans for the December 28, 2005, murder of Steven Kennedy, another Katrina evacuee who had relocated to Houston.

Police say the killing was in revenge for the 2003 murder of James "Soulja Slim" Tapp Jr., a Louisiana rapper.

…And they continue to self-destruct.

Today, March 23, 2006, I went and sat with Miss Harriett. She happened to catch me at home and I wanted to go by and check on her.

She wasn't feeling well and informed me that she'd be having surgery on her back within the next few days. She also stated that she has three tumors on one kidney and one on the other.

This bad news was compounded when she told me of how she received word that her brother's son, Dwayne Bailey had been stabbed in the back on February 21, 2006.

It would be three days later before he was seen and treated at a local hospital. On February 25, 2006, he would die from complications associated with that injury.

His sister has pressed authorities to investigate the circumstances surrounding his stabbing and eventual death and she was assured that they would follow up and confer with her. She's still waiting.

"Nobody cares about us Shan. The media has people thinking that Katrina evacuees are the cause for everything bad that's happened and they just don't care. The Red Cross had trucks on every corner in New Orleans and there wasn't a black face on any of them. The food was bad and was the cause of many people getting sick. They didn't seem genuinely concerned about us. You know they're still finding bodies and we'll never know a real count. Shan, nobody cares and we'll never be OK again. If I make it through my surgery, you'll be here won't you?"

I listened to Miss Harriett as she voiced more concerns and I smiled to let her know that I was paying attention.

"Miss Harriett, the media can say all that they want to about you all, but there are many of us who know better and we aren't letting them get away with it. There are many that care about you all and I'm sure you've seen it by their actions. Don't be discouraged. Yes, after you have your surgery, I'll be here."

When Katrina Stood Down, We Came Running, but Rita Tripped Us

Today, March 24, 2006, three more Hurricane Katrina evacuees were killed in Houston, Texas. Two were shot and killed at an apartment complex on the Southwest side of town; one was found inside an apartment and the other was found in the courtyard of the complex.

A friend stated that one of them had mentioned their getting into an argument with someone, but she was not told of their identity or anything else related to the incident. Now, she's left wondering whether it was anything worth their dying over.

The other murder would take place on the North side of town, at a motel. Although there was two people shot, only one died (at the time of the news report). He died inside the apartment and the other jumped through a widow after being shot and was hospitalized in serious condition.

Houston Police Officials have met with the FBI and are trying desperately to get a handle on the escalating murder rate and the whereabouts of the known "criminal element" that may have come in via New Orleans evacuees. The murder rate is currently at eighty-five. Last year, this same time, it was at fifty-nine.

The timing couldn't have been any worse for a World News Tonight broadcast, Elizabeth Vargas would report that an internal memo of the Red Cross concludes that half of the 3.7 billion dollars that was collected for Hurricane Katrina relief efforts was "mismanaged."

An itemized record shows laptop computers, cell phones, and a vehicle went unaccounted for, not to mention that donated cots had been "rented" to those seeking them.

The brighter side to the news broadcasts for the day would be that two hundred fifty Howard University students were named "Persons of the Week."

World News Tonight bestowed this honor on them for making the supreme humanitarian gesture of going to New

Orleans on their Spring Break and gutting homes that could be rebuilt.

A student spoke of how lively and festive they were as they rode the buses there and how total silence fell over them as they entered New Orleans and witnessed first hand the devastation that took place only months ago.

Many were obviously unprepared for the sight. Their wide eyes, looks of disbelief, and eventual tears would bring this reality a little closer to home for them.

They suited up in the protective gear that is required of anyone who will be participating in any acts of rebuilding and set about the task of helping those who are still hopeful that their homes in New Orleans will again become "livable."

Students of Howard University, I too salute your efforts and know that what you saw has had a deep impact on you and will further drive you to initiate a change that will alleviate some of the most preventable mistakes and corruption that Hurricane Katrina brought to light. May God bless and keep you all.

The Faces of Hurricanes Katrina and Rita

Mary Jones

Bridget and Keith Cloud and Family

Unidentified woman and niece at donation drop site.

Three unidentified evacuees of Katrina resting on lawn
near Reliant Stadium.

Unidentified man resting at donation site, near Reliant Stadium.

Karl Jones

Isaiah and Deborah Johnson and sons Derrick and Chris

Theresa Ward and daughter Diamondneeshay

Harriett Butler

**Brenda Parker and her father, Gordon, and her children
Derek, Destiny, Brendien**

Photographical Diary

**Empty grocery shelves and anxious customers,
preparing for Rita's approach.**

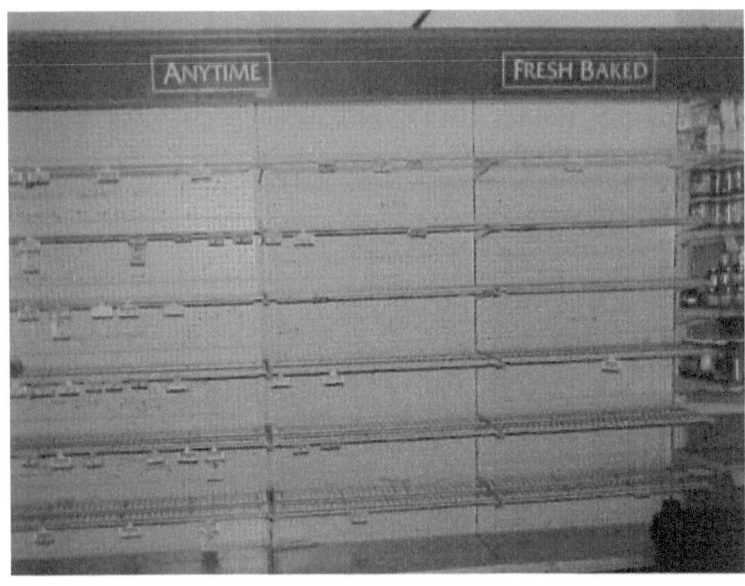

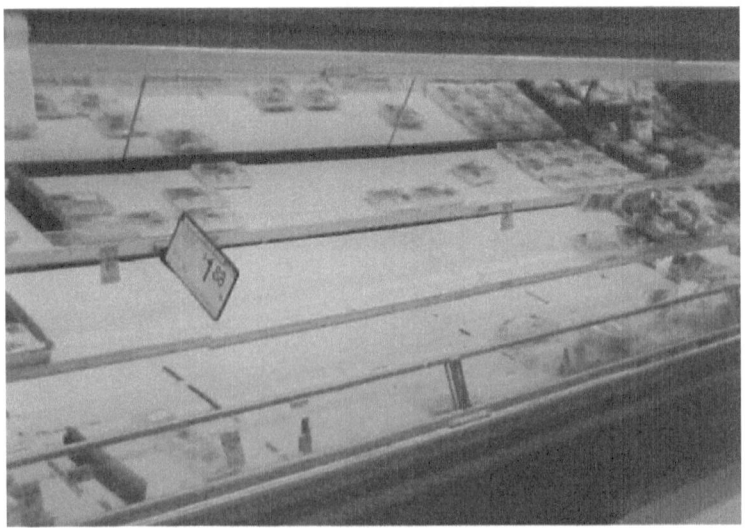

Cars backed up to get on SH 290, in Houston, Texas, as Rita approaches. The woman in the bottom picture was forced to use the restroom on the side of the road, for fear of having to give up her place in the already long line.

Volunteers sorting, bagging, and preparing donated goods for evacuees of Katrina, who were within walking distance from Reliant Stadium and the Astrodome.

Donation Drive at the Breakfast Klub

Congresswoman Sheila Jackson-Lee, interviewing with a local television station, during a donation drive at the Breakfast Klub, the Sunday before Labor Day.

**Volunteers at the Breakfast Klub the Sunday before
Labor Day sorting, bagging, and labeling
donated goods.**

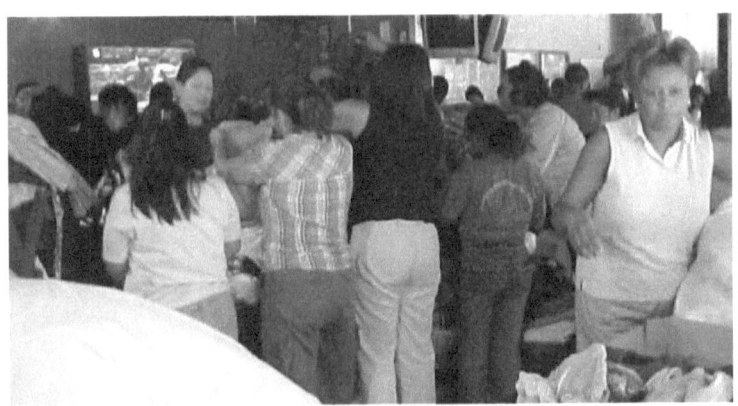

Author Shandra Love.

At a shelter during the anticipation of Hurricane Rita –
September 24, 2005. Some unidentified children still
celebrated birthdays with a cake and refreshments
donated by volunteers.

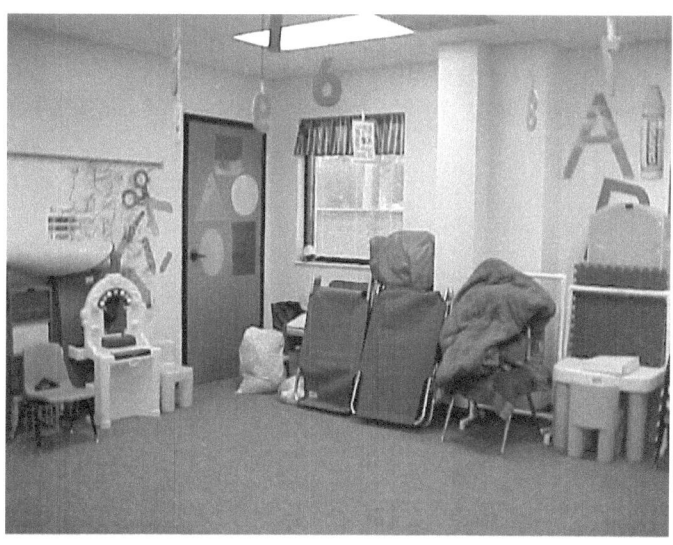

The approach and aftermath of Hurricane Rita. Dark clouds, downed power line, snapped tree, <u>beautiful dawn sky</u>.